Queen Mother

Dorothy Woods

Queen Mother
Copyright © 2023 by Dorothy Woods

Library of Congress Control Number: 2022923816
ISBN-13: Paperback: 978-1-64749-880-1
        ePub: 978-1-64749-829-0

All rights reserved. No part of this publication may be reproduced, distributed, or transmitted in any form or by any means, including photocopying, recording, or other electronic or mechanical methods, without the prior written permission of the publisher or author, except in the case of brief quotations embodied in critical reviews and certain other noncommercial uses permitted by copyright law.

Although every precaution has been taken to verify the accuracy of the information contained herein, the author and publisher assume no responsibility for any errors or omissions. No liability is assumed for damages that may result from the use of information contained within.

Printed in the United States of America

GoToPublish LLC
1-888-337-1724
www.gotopublish.com
info@gotopublish.com

CONTENTS

Chapter 1	New Beginnings	1
Chapter 2	My Personal Calvary	11
Chapter 3	Life in Prison	21
Chapter 4	The Devil's Work	31
Chapter 5	Answered Prayer	41
Chapter 6	Picking Up The Pieces	45
Chapter 7	Entrapment	51
Chapter 8	Starting Over Again	57
Chapter 9	Family Reunification	69

CHAPTER 1

New Beginnings

Digging my feet into the unknown depths of the warm Jamaican sand, I stared at my feet, watching the white granules filter between my toes. Not seeing, but lost in my thoughts. My time had finally arrived.

Two escorts; one female and one male officer, shielded me from the front. The other escort followed me from the back as we exited the airplane onto the tarmac. If the electrical excitement in the air could be measured in physical terms, it would have to be a runaway heartbeat, ready to burst my chest.

Quickly surveying my surroundings, I made a mental note of the various travellers, scurrying to their next destination or rushing into the arms of their loved ones, all of them getting on with their lives.

Following the procession of people, accompanied by my escorts, we started toward the escalators at the far end of the terminal. The sudden flashes of light broke into the tranquillity of our stroll. As the raging sea of reporters converged on me and my plain-clothed escorts, I was blinded by the non-stop flashing lights, as the reporter's strobe continued to pop like fireworks on the fourth of July.

Microphones pushed into my face, rapid fire demands started coming in the form of questions.

"Did you think you'd get away with it?"

"No comments!"

"How many kids did you claim?"

"No comments!"

The human surge of reporters and the mass of electronic equipment, microphones and television cameras, encumbered our confident stride into an immobile state.

Methodically weaving our way through the media paparazzi, we stepped onto the down escalator toward the main doors of Los Angeles International Airport; overzealous reporters enjoying the chase.

"How much money did you get?"

"No comments!"

"Did you believe that you would be caught?"

"No comments!"

Spilling onto the ground level, the main doors loomed ahead. An escape from the curious public and from the swelling ocean of reporters. My demeanour, always composed, well-practiced smile and gracious manner, clothed my being.

"Who is she?"

"Do you recognize her?"

Our snail's pace continued. Was I really that news worthy? The unmarked vehicle parked at the curb was in my sight.

"Let us through!"

"Excuse us. Move out of the way!" were the commands of my escorts.

Never relenting in their pursuit, the mass surrounded the awaiting car. Sitting my small frame on the back seat, I felt the beating of my heart. Settling into a normal rhythm, breathing became easier. Breathing through my nose… exhaling through my mouth.

The swarm surrounded the car like angry bees attracted to the sweet nectar of a flower in bloom.

Edging the car into the flow of airport traffic away from the disbanding mass, we began our mid-day travel into downtown Los Angeles. As if we were escaping, the now mobile swarm of reporters began to flee the scene, hitching rides in awaiting network vehicles in hot pursuit.

So this is what authorities would dub a box office success. Well staged. Well executed. The media taking the bait were anxiously awaiting the "Queens" court house arrival. Carnage and commotion created utter mayhem in the court house and court room, the noise echoing in the hallways.

Descending into the dark bowels of the underground park garage, the blackness and silence enveloped us. Tires screeching on turns brought me out of the depths of my thoughts.

Assisted from the comfort and security of the car, I was escorted into a small waiting room that would be my access into the court room. Sitting on a wooden straight back chair, I was tethered to the chair with handcuffs, one cuff on my left wrist, one to the chair, waiting… and waiting.

The bailiff released my stainless tether to the chair, he led me into the pandemonium in the hallway. Another tidal of anxious media. Questions. Flashing bulbs. Microphones. No comments!

The interior court room was tranquil, the Judge in command silencing the court room with his stare. Media vultures were seated through-out the viewing galley. Handing on my every movement and word being directed up the centre aisle, all eyes were on me. I surveyed the spectators. My gaze came to rest on my husband, Billy, stoically sitting on the bench opposite me, flanked with two attorneys.

Dumbfounded by his non-responsive manner towards me, I was seated next to my counsel, another ring in the ongoing-circus. The grand finale.

"State of California Versus Dorothy Woods and Billy Woods," announced the clerk.

Announcing the charges, the clerk asked how I pled.

"Not guilty!" I replied as my attorney nodded.

Quarter of a million dollars was my bail; Billy's only ten thousand dollars.

Knowing that a blanket lien had been placed on all assets, the prospect of my bail was non-existent. An acquaintance fronted his home; Billy was released two hours later.

My moment in the judicial spotlight was short lived. Photographers and media personal scrambled toward the court room exits, waiting for the opportunity to interview and shoot footage of the "Welfare Queen." Knowing that photographs were prohibited in the court room, a bottleneck was created at the exit. The bailiff rushing and shoving through the crowd, bodies pressing in on all sides. The noise level rising in frequent pitches. Inside the confines of safety in the holding room, I was again tethered to the chair.

Having no concept of time, what felt like hours, but in reality, only minutes ticked by as I was moved into a large holding cell. Looking through the open bars were steel benches lining the cell. Women crammed the benches, sitting and lying down, sleeping, and some simply sitting and contemplating their own demise.

A flurry of activity brought us to our feet; five or six uniformed officers appeared outside the cell. Without the restraints of handcuffs, we were all moved down a hallway that led to the parking garage. An olive drab green school bus was our transportation to Sybil Brand Institution (SBI) in another location within the Los Angeles Metropolitan area.

Forming a single line, we each entered the bus. As I climbed the steps to the bus, I came face to face with two cages, each with two benches housing violent offenders, murderers, and kidnappers; that type of person. The bus was filled from the back; first in, last off. Not knowing that "new fish" were to remain on the bus, I was in the middle of the incoming line. A new fish is a new inmate, not schooled yet in the rules and regulations of jail protocol.

Within a half hour, we arrived at SBI, where the driver announced that everyone was to get off the bus, the exception being all "new fish". Realizing I was "new fish," I felt like a minnow amongst the sharks. I swam within the confines of the bus as I waited. I was swimming in my thoughts to pass the long wait. After treading water for over two hours, I was released into a large tank, another holding cell for new commits to be processed.

The large stocky female officer yelled her commands in a deep guttural tone.

"Give me your left hand!"

Roughly jerking each of my hands, I was fingerprinted. Wiping the unremovable ink from my hands was impossible. No soap and water. A lone dry paper towel.

The next barking order:

"Place your feet on the line on the floor!"

The toes of my dress shoes on the yellow line; I looked up into the camera as the barking officer dismissed me, ready to fry the next fish, my picture having been taken.

The string of new fish were shuffled into a large greyish room. Dimly lit from overhead, we were ordered into doorless stalls. The stainless steel environment of our stalls echoed the hurried movements of women stripping, the beginning of the end of my dignity. Then, like a drill sergeant, the non-stop barking began:

"Take off all you clothes!"

"Do you have a hairpiece?"

"If you do have a hairpiece, take it out of your hair!"

"Throw all clothes into a pile on the floor!"

The two female officers on a search and destroy mission began their verbal assault.

"Run your fingers and hands through your hair!"

Not accepting a casual raking of my hair, I was ordered to extend my fingers through the length of my hair, away from ears. My hair was standing in various spikes all over my head, like I had seen a ghost.

Not being accustomed to exposing myself in vulgar manners was the most dehumanizing experience ever. Each stall was ordered to perform various physical maneuvers. Having had 13 children, I had never felt I had lost my dignity or my modesty. The continual close and repeated personal inspection of every possible crevice of my being were violated in the incoming process.

Standing within my stainless stall, facing the wall, the officers rang out:

"Place your feet shoulder width!"

Each stall following the command, the two officers walked a line, stopping at each stall to further give commands.

"Bend over and spread those cheeks!"

"Squat and cough three times!"

"Spread those vaginas!"

Not always being satisfied with a particular individual's performance, the officer would demand the individual to repeat the squatting, coughing, and spreading routine again and again until they were satisfied at the level of exposure.

My last shreds of dignity ripped from me. I held my tears that were burning my eyes. The rock I wanted to crawl under would never be big enough to cover the loss I felt.

I was provided a pair of ladies panties, one bar, a blue shift dress, and a pair of shower shoes. The pile of discarded clothes were placed in a jail bag. All bags were tagged, collected, and put into storage by the trustee.

As a group, we were escorted into a holding cell. Looking at each other we were clones, same everything except our faces. Another hurry and wait situation. Slowly the names were barked out. Removing those individuals to be escorted by trustees to their assigned dorms.

Waiting and waiting. All alone for the next three hours. Weariness overcame me. Jet lag, my trip from Miami to Los Angeles. The constant hubbub of reporters, court appearances, shuffling from cell to cell, enduring the emotional rejection of my husband, Billy, the degrading manner and treatment by the officers... Sleep overcame me, temporarily.

"Woods!"

"Let's!"

Shaking the very much-needed sleep from my befuddled mind, I followed the officer. I was walking down a long corridor. Open and empty cells on the right, a loud clanking sound released the lock mechanism within the barred door. The officer grabbed the long door handle and swung the door open, motioning me in with her hand. Securing the door, the hard slamming bar door jolted me to the bone.

Dazed by isolation and Billy's rejection, the tears came. Uncontrollable tears and sobbing racked my already weary body. The desire to die overwhelmed me. I wanted to die. Frames of footage ran through my head. All that Billy and I had gone through. I worshipped him. My Savior. My deliverer. How cruel he was to abandon me. How could I live?

Four days, my state of emotional distress consumed me, only leaving my cell for thirty minutes each night to shower. I remained in isolation.

Metallic sounds echoed in my cell, the door sliding open standing around in the center of my humble surrounding. I could hear a faint calling of my name.

"Woods."

"Come to the front!"

Stepping from within the cell I curiously approached the stout figure at the end of the corridor. Wondering who in the world could this be? What could she want? Why would she want me?

Standing about five-three, her sandy blonde hair framed her large blue eyes. Approaching the bars I kept looking at the angelic pixie before me.

"I'm chaplain Jones, the chaplain here! I saw on the movement sheet that you are housed here! I came to bring you a bible."

"Thank you very much!" I said as I took the black bible.

"I encourage you to start reading in the book of John. If you have any questions I'm available. If there is anything I can do for you, just come see me!"

Surprised at her comment I responded, "Oh! They won't let me do anything in here!"

She exclaimed. "They can't keep you from me. They can't keep you from seeing me if you want to. All you have to do is fill out a request. If you request it, they have to bring you to see me."

Holding the bible in my hands I pressed it into my heart. I felt amazed that a total stranger cared for me. Turning to leave, chaplain Jones says, "Enjoy your bible!"

Returning to my cell, I could physically and emotionally feel the weight lifting.

My dinky, six by six, iron-barred environment, was very humbling. My cell had two steel framed bunks, the center of each frame had spring, supports, and a thin mattress. Lavatory facilities were a piece stainless steel unit, where the tank on a regular toilet is, that was now where the bathroom sink, was located. There were two push buttons, one to the left of the sink flushed the toilet; the other button next to the sink spout was utilized for sink and drinking water.

Sitting on the lower bunk in my cell I opened my new possessor. I had no pre-conceived idea what this book would contain or the magnitude of change it would bring to my life. Following chaplain Jones' instructions, I began reading the gospel of John.

The words of the pages before me came to life, as if jumping from the pages they were written on. They became real, something tangible. I experienced a joy and peace that was indescribable. I realized that Jesus loved me. Someone cared for me; for me, just me, not what I could do or give to them. The feeling of despair evaporated.

Over the next few days, I read the book of John over and over. Twenty-one chapters, approximately a dozen times. Excitement bubbling over at my new found hope and source of unconditional love. I had to see the chaplain.

Knowing many of these beautiful books had adorned my house! A bible in almost every room. Expensive leather-bound volumes. The best money could buy. How silly? All this time I had looked at them as "Good Luck Charms," like a rabbit's foot, as if it would bring me good luck, and everybody could use good luck!

My first visit on a Wednesday proved to be very interesting. The officer escort left me in her cramped four-by-six office. Her desk faced the door. A little small cane chair at the end of the desk, and a simple bookcase next to the visitor chair, contained vast volumes of spiritual information. My spiritual appetite had been awakened by pouring over the book of John. It is no longer dormant. I was thirsty for his love and hungry for his word.

Chaplain Jones sat silently in her chair listening to me incessantly chatter about what I had learned about Jesus. I couldn't put into words the joy and tears I had just reading the scriptures. I needed to know if what I was feeling was normal.

"I read that Jesus loves me!"

"Are you saved?" she asked me

"Ya! I go to church and I've been baptized," I answered.

Chuckling at my response, she had heard so many people profess that before.

"Have you ever asked the Lord into your heart?"

"What is that?"

"I believed that when the pastor said that the door of the church is open, and when I walked down that aisle and shook his hands, that made me saved."

The chaplain dropped her head and smiled.

"Well, I continued to attend church. Didn't that help to keep me saved? I didn't have to worry about reading the bible of repenting, I thought. Now I see I was wrong." I explained.

Then chaplain Jones said, "My people are destroyed for lack of knowledge. Hosea 3:6"

The shoe sure fit. I was wearing it. That was what was happening to me.

Taking her bible, we began to explore Romans, the plan of salvation.

"For all have sinned and come short of the glory of God. Romans 3:23"

"For the wages of sin is death, but the gift of God is eternal life. Romans 6:23"

"If thou shall confess with thy mouth the Lord Jesus, and believe in thy heart the God has raised him from the dead thou shall be saved. Romans 10:9"

"For with the heart man believe unto righteousness and with the mouth confession is made unto salvation. Romans 10:10"

The abundance of wisdom overflowed into me, absorbing it like a sponge, spiritually saturated. Full.

The chaplain begin to minister to me. "Dorothy, salvation and being saved is the same thing. They are interchangeable. Being saved is like your ABC's.

A. Accept what you read in John. You saw that you were a sinner, and in need of a Savior. You have read in the book of John that Jesus is the Savior of the world.

B. Believing in your heart that God raised Jesus from the dead. That He is alive, and present with us.

C. Confess Him. Pray to him and ask Him to take control of your life."

Then she took my hands and asked, "Are you ready?"

Never realizing that I needed or wanted salvation, I wanted this. Like a thirst, salvation was going to quench my thirst.

Holding my hands, and with my eyes closed, the Chaplain began to pray the sinner's prayer.

Focusing and concentration on her words, I prayed the sinner's prayer.

"Father, I am a sinner.
I need a Savior.

I believe that Jesus died on the cross for me.
Forgive me of my sins.
Come into my heart, and save me.
Thank you for coming into my heart. Amen."

"Welcome to the family of God!" the Chaplain said and she gave me a big hug.

The dam of tears fell over onto my cheeks. Such joy, unspeakable. Happiness. Happy that I had a family. How simple it was to ask and receive this joy. Like chaplain Jones said, it's as simple as ABC. I was so appreciative that God would accept me. I found Him!

Escorted back to my cell, I felt I could conquer the world.

"We are more than conquers through Him that loved us. Romans 8:37"

What had tormented me at night, dwelling on my loss of possessions, the things that had taken years to accumulate? I would do anything to get and do anything to keep these material possessions. Now here I am, losing these things, and there is no way to hold onto them. It was driving me insane. I can't hold onto them. I am locked up with no one who cares about me. I felt that those things made me somebody.

Now I could release those material possessions. Let them go. I now had Jesus.

"But my God shall supply all your needs according to
His riches and glory by Christ Jesus.
Philippians 4:10"

I had reason to live.

The Bible became my constant companion, starting to read the New Testament, from Matthew through Revelations, sometimes in one day, reading His words over and over again, like food for my spiritual hunger; wanting more.

After my initial meeting with the chaplain, I began to meet with her three times a week. I was enrolled in a bible course. She instructed a discipleship class of four female inmates. We had one-on-one contact for spiritual development. I was transferred to the general population two weeks into my discipleship studies.

CHAPTER 2

My Personal Calvary

> "Take my yoke upon you and learn of me,
> for I am meek and lowly in heart,
> and ye shall fine rest unto your soul (v29)
> For my yoke is easy and my burden is light."
> **Matthew 11:29&30**

I take up my cross and leave my burden of solitary confinement. His goodness is so great. I can't always understand. He had broken my bonds, and in Him I am free. My spirit soared to new heights. Just like he promised, he would share all my sorrows. He'd be there for all of us tomorrow. Jesus was here to stay.

How many times had He been knocking on my heart's door? His love loosed my chains and now in Him I'm free. My Savior had opened all the right doors.

"Behold! I stand at the door and knock. If any man hear my voice, and open the door, I will come into him, and sup with him, and he with me. Revelations 3:20"

Every day since that fateful Wednesday, I've feasted with the Lord. Every morning!

During the day, and each night, always glorifying His name in praise and thanksgiving amen!

I was no longer isolated from the other inmates. Praise God! My new home was in a pod of cells called "High Power." Each cell within this pod housed two female inmates. High power meant that the females within this pod had a high bail or no bail. High-level crimes.

The freedom within this pod was wondrous. I could move about the entire block. There was a day room that had a television. I could hear and see what was going on in the world. Another isolation barrier was lifted.

All meals were eaten away from the pod. We would line up and walk down two ramps, not stairs, to the general dining room. We shuffled single file through the line; we were each handed a tray, cafeteria style. No choice of likes or dislikes. Correctional officers, nothing nice or pleasant to speak of, barked commands.

"Four people to a table!"

"No talking to others around you!"

Seating four people to a table, with round stainless steel tables and stools, bolted to the floor. We were allowed to talk in hushed tones to only those seated at our table. Food bartering was allowed at our table only. Those caught bartering outside their assigned table were immediately removed from the dining room, given their meal, and placed in the lock-up for disciplinary action.

I learned quickly to eat the unidentifiable four basic food groups in fifteen minutes or less. Food was prohibited from leaving the dining room.

Inmates could purchase snack and candy items, in addition to personal toiletry items from the commissary cart on Tuesdays and Fridays.

All new incoming inmates received a personal care package, which consisted of soap, toothpaste, toothbrush, deodorant, shampoo, and a comb. After these items were gone, we were expected to purchase these items from the commissary.

Visiting friends and family could bring money to inmates in the form of cash or money in order to purchase commissary items.

The Lord had loosened my chains. I could get a pass and walk to and from my pod to the Chaplain's office, less the handcuffs. Freedom in the smallest sense.

> "Trust in the Lord with all thine heart, and lean not unto thine own understanding. (v5)
> In all thy ways acknowledge him, and he shall direct thy paths."
> **Proverbs 3:5&6**

Feeling and believing His word and promises my spirit was further up lifted every day to new heights of peace and joy. Each day began with His word, Psalm 23

> "The Lord is my shepherd I shall not want.
> He maketh me to lie down in green pastures: he

leadeth me beside still waters.
He restouth my soul: he leadeth me in the path
of righteousness for his name sake.
Yea though I walk through the valley of the
shadow of death, I will fear no evil. For thou
art with me; thy rod and thy staff they comfort me.
Thou preparest a table before me in the
presence of mine enemies, thou anointest my head
with oil; my cup runneth over.
Surely goodness and mercy shall follow me all
the days of my life; and I will dwell in the
house of the Lord forever.'
Psalm 23

Anxious to share what had set me free, the message of God's love, of hope, His promises, and the spirit of peace that passes all understanding, I began to witness to the other inmates; sharing Jesus.

All the stories that I heard became the same. Absolutely no one person was in this jail because of their own doing or fault. Imagine all these inmates; people incarcerated.

"I'm here because it's my husband's fault!"
"I'm here because my father raped me when I was a little girl!"
"I'm here because it's my families fault!"
"I'm here because it's my neighbour's fault!"
"I'm here because it's the police's fault!"
"He that covet his sins shall not prosper; but who so
confesses and forsakes them shall have mercy.
Proverbs 28:13"

People don't want to admit their own faults. Looking within ourselves is often too hurtful, and revealing. We're afraid of ourselves. We might not like what we see. The Spirit spoke to me, revealing:

"I was here because it was "my" fault, no one else's."

My, that was a hard pill to swallow for me. Yet I had to confess this and accept the responsibility of my own actions; no matter how painful it would be for me. Remembering that my Lord and Savior is merciful and forgiving.

My outlook on my situation took on a whole new persona. I was positive. Hope had come alive in me. My being exuded joy. Inmates perplexed by the change in me took notice. Sharing and accepting the word of God had changed me.

"When I read the bible, it doesn't do anything for me. I don't understand what I'm supposed to feel or know," said one of the women during one of the bible study sessions.

After taking this into consideration, I headed up a bible study group each day for those inmates interested in learning His word.

Meeting after breakfast each morning, four of us met in my cell, beginning with the gospel of John. We would read one passage and I explained what it meant. Standing in my small cell we'd stand and have a group prayer. I taught them old gospel songs.

"Soon and very soon we're going to see the King!
Amazing Grace! and
What a friend we have in Jesus."

Before leaving my cell during our first meeting I led the three ladies to the Lord, reciting the sinner's prayer.

> "Jesus answered and said unto him, verily, verily, I say
> unto thee, except a man be born again, he cannot see the
> kingdom of God.
> **John 3:3**"

The following morning, the change in these women was apparent. The manner in which they carried themselves, the tone of their voices, radiated a glow on their faces. They were waiting in my cell for the word, bibles in hand. The chaplain continued to provide bibles as our study group grew. After the first month of studying the book of John, we continued on in the New Testament to the book of Matthew. We wanted to cover the entire New Testament, so we did.

Our group had now grown to ten women; all hungry for the word. The lesson of forgiveness that I was ministering on really impacted me.

> "For if ye forgive men their trespasses,
> your heavenly Father will also forgive you. (v14)
> But if ye forgive not men their trespasses neither will
> your Father forgive your trespasses."
> **Matthew 6:14 & 15.**

So many of those women, myself included, had such terrible things happened to them. They were hurt so badly, with their spouse, friends, and family. Battered and beaten. Molested. How could they forgive the people who had inflected such a deep hurt?

I began to search my inner being. I had stopped blaming my friend Ruth, but had I forgiven her? Realizing that I had not totally forgiven her, I had to make amends.

Dialling Ruth's number I felt fear and anxiety.

"Would she answer the phone?

Would she accept my forgiveness?

Would she be angry?"

The phone ringing in my ear, I held my breath. Ruth answered the telephone.

"Hello?"

"Hi Ruth, this is Dorothy."

The silence so thick you could almost see and feel it. A deliberate and sarcastic response.

"Yes! What do you want?"

"I am just calling to say I forgive you, and I have no hard feelings against you anymore."

Never anticipating her response, I was assaulted with a barrage of accusations.

"This is a trick! You're trying to trick me. Yes you are tricking me. What are you trying to do to me?"

Ruth continued to repeatedly scream into the telephone, as if she was possessed, a mad woman.

Reassuring her, I found I couldn't get a word in edge wise, only inciting her further. And suddenly as the telephone rang, it went dead. The sound resounding in my ear.

Dumbfounded by Ruth's reaction I could only stare at the dead receiver in my hand. Hanging up the telephone, I knew what I had to do. Minister His word.

Continuing to minister His word, our group continued to grow. Even as we grew in wisdom and in numbers, we still had the enemy amongst us. Non-participants of the study group became antagonistic.

"You're a criminal. How could you teach a bible study group?

It's nothing but jail house religion!

God ain't gonna listen to you. You're all hypocrites!

You all come to jail and use God as a crutch!

What gives you the right and authority to teach the bible?"

Seeing the change in the women in the study group, I stood fast in my commitment to minister His word, even amongst the adversaries.

"Be sober, be vigilant; because your adversary the devil, as a roaring lion, walketh about seeking whom he may devour. Peter 5:8"

We had to stand united. If we don't stand for something, we'll fall for anything. Praise God we stood together. Our adversaries proudly professed their sinful ways. Their links to drugs, prostitution, pimps, and crime… hours of non-stop bragging about being bad and their addictions always embellishing their own story to make it look "badder" than the next person.

Not only were the inmates our adversaries, the correction officers were, too; I should say, some of them. Occasionally an officer would disband our group, sighting;

"You could be plotting against the establishment!"

The growing size of the group seemed to anger the officers. I was given several verbal warnings.

"This is the chaplain's job. That's what she gets paid for! She's qualified; you're are not! Look at you, you're locked up. You're not qualified. I'm going to see if you'll be smiling when the Judge slap you with all that time!"

I was warned to stop the studies, because once I was sentenced I wouldn't be thinking about my bible or any bible study. The harassment continued; random searches of my cell and belongs, my bible was taken many times. The officer throwing it to the floor at times, no regard for the Lord's word.

One particular Friday was a search of our pod and cells. The same group of officers that had been harassing me about disbanding the bible study, were conducting the search. All the inmates were escorted into the dayroom, while the officers ransacked the cells. The officer yelled out my name.

"Woods!"

Responding to their command, I came forward.

"Yes," I answered.

"You're going to lock-up!"

"Lock-up! For what?"

Smiling smugly, "Flatware from the dining room under your mattress!"

Placing my hands behind my back, I was handcuffed.

"May I have my bible?"

"No! You can't have no bible. Nothing in lock-up!"

I was placed in a cell isolated from other inmates, pending my hearing. All privileges were taken away. Commissary, dining room, and day room. My food was brought to me three times a day on a cart, eating all meals in my cell. No television. No bible.

Since I was in pending lock-up, I was able to make my weekly telephone call. Using that call wisely, I called Rev. Smith. I advised him of my situation and asked him would he call the watch commander and ask him to bring me a bible down to me.

This incident happening on a Friday, I knew I've spent the weekend in pending lock-up. Monday or Tuesday, the council would hear the incident and pass sentence. Similar to a regular court system, I would be found guilty or not guilty.

Like Daniel, I believed that God would be faithful and deliver me. Tuesday morning, I went before the council; a lieutenant, and two senior Deputies. The lieutenant read the incident report, and what I was charged with, asking me what I had to say about those charges.

I told the lieutenant, "I don't know how the flatware got under my mattress, sir! I can tell you this sir, I did not bring that flatware from the dining room. The first of my knowledge of the flatware was when I was on my way to lock-up, sir!"

They sent me out of the room, and had a meeting with each other. After fifteen minutes, they sent for me.

"We believe you, you are not guilty. You may go back to your regular housing. Not guilty!" the lieutenant stated.

I felt victorious. God had come through for me, standing firm in my belief. I could get back to our bible study group. In my absence, the women were fearful of the abuse I received, not wanting to take on the challenge. Their faith had not matured enough to step up to the leadership helm in my absence.

Even though I was saved, I still had worry and anxiety about my five small children, stair steps. Knowing that Billy had a drinking problem, I was sure that they would die without me.

Our first unseen visit in two months since my incarceration. I was geared up. My children would be overwhelmed. They would be distraught. Larry, my adult son, sat across from me. Through the Plexiglas, he picks up the phone.

"Hi mom! How are you?"

In utter amazement, I realized my children were making it without me. Running around the visit area, chasing each other. Laughing. Pulling on the phone, wanting to talk.

I was crushed. They were surviving without me. All this time, the inner turmoil I felt… they were getting along without me.

Walking back to my cell block, I felt hurt. My hurt turning to anger. I wasn't needed like I thought. A mixed bag of emotions. The tears of hurt stung my eyes. I felt I was their life support. We made each other whole. How wrong I was, because God was their life support, not me.

The occasional visits with the children were far and few between. When we did have visits, I would minister to Billy and the children, telling them about Jesus, and how the bible study was growing, and how I had seen so many women lives change.

The visits stopped abruptly. Writing my family inquiring as to why Billy and the children had not returned for a visit, and no word from them. No response to my letters and calls. Even in the court room, Billy didn't acknowledge me.

In speaking with my family, I found that Billy had indicated to them that I had gone crazy.

I was referred to as a Jesus freak. Billy had decided not to come back or let the children keep doing my work.

Feeling weak physically, a warmth blanketed me. I felt faint, laying back in my bed spell bound I replayed the voice I heard over in my mind.

"What had I witnessed?"

Never having had a vision before I was sure it was God. The unexplainable peace was within my spirit. At peace, gaining my composure, I checked to see if my roommate had heard or seen this event. She was fast asleep.

After this experience I felt I had received a revelation in knowledge. I could now see things in the bible, enabling me to explain His word in a greater degree.

Nothing changed in my home life with Billy and the children. But the Lord had given me peace. He was my friend. I had heard the word and seen the light. I was able to release Billy.

Continuing with the Lord word, the bible study grew. The enthusiasm and momentum was high. The chaplain would say, "Revival in cell block 4200!"

Seeing the positive influence and good work in the "High Power" pod, the chaplain arranged a celebration and special service in the main dining room, to which all inmates attended. All Protestant church services throughout the facility were invited. I was recognized by the chaplain for my outstanding work and achievements in ministering the word to the inmates in cell block 4200. Seeing the growth of the bible study correspondence, new converts, and the level of attendance at church services, was at an all-time high.

This celebration news spread like wildfire. More and more women were hungry for a relationship with the Lord. Accommodating the growing number was becoming more difficult as the days progress. A miracle from heaven. The watch commander seeing the growth permitted me to use the day room for one hour each morning, 8 o'clock to 9 o'clock A.M., for bible studies, before the 4200 population regular activates.

CHAPTER 3

Life in Prison

March 1983. I arrived at California Institution for Women in Frontera, California. It's the only structure in the town. There are no other residents living in the town. The town consists only of prisoners. It's located near the Ontario airport. The prison is situated on a vast amount of land, with incredible landscapes. Trees line the streets that lead to the dozen buildings that was sprawl over the prison compound. The view was magnificent. It was like being away in college campus.

However, the inmates were not like college students. Ninety percent of the inmates were serving time for narcotics related charges. They were junkies, pushers, prostitutes, and characters from a whole different world than where I came from. Then too, the inmates acted if they had come to a "gay farm." They walked around as if they had been attacked by vampire. They paired up like husband and wife. Many of the women shaved off their hair, looking just like men. They called each other:

"My woman! My wife! And my old lady!"

This was the norm.

The question kept running through my mind.

"What am I doing here?"

I didn't fit the profile of the average prisoners. Depression settled over me as I gazed at the population.

I lived in Harrison's cottage. I was placed on the long-termers wing with 100 other women. Twenty-five of them were Spanish, ten were white, and the rest were black. I had always gotten along well with people because most of them came from the county jail (SBI), where I had lived for the past two years. However, when they entered C.I.W., most of them changed like night and day. In this situation, they were different; this was an environment.

The bible study in the county jail acted as if they had never heard of Jesus.

There was a 30-day processing period in the institution: everyone had to be evaluated. No one could be idle; one had to work or go to school. We had to be cleared medically, and we also had to take a proficiency test.

The first week, I had to do all my medical examinations. The second week, I had to go to the dentist. The third week, I had my eyes tested. Then, last of all, I took my proficient test.

While waiting for all my test results to come in, I started seeking employment, so that on the date of my classification interview, I could tell the committee where I wanted to work.

Everyone wore their own clothes, but upon our arrival we were given state issue clothing because we have to send home for our personal clothing. For twenty days in prison, I went to my friend's room to borrow some of her clothes to wear until I received my box of clothing from home. Her name was Ann.

"As I settle into this prison routine, I see everybody wearing their own clothes, so will you loan me a couple outfits to wear until my box come from home?" I asked.

"You're welcome to look through my things, and if there is anything you can use, you are welcome to have them," she replied.

Ten minutes later I was picking out the outfits. Unfortunately, most of her clothes were too small for me, but I was able to use three outfits sufficiently. Gratefully, I accepted the loan of the outfits, so I didn't have to wear that state issue clothing.

"I am trying to find a job assignment before I go before the classification committee. Where do you work? Do they have any opening now?" I inquired of her.

"Hard going!" she said as she sat on her bed. "I work in the kitchen, and its hard work. I don't want you to have to work there!" she explained.

"Heavens! This is prison! If you can do the work, I can do it too," I snarled.

"Well, to put it lightly, you was doing a great work at S.B.I. That ministry is very much needed in here. But let me give you some good advice. Do your own time one day at a time. Watch your back! Be careful who you talk to. Keep a low profile! There are more drugs in here than on the streets!" She informed me, frowning as she rose from the bedside.

"What? It's not that bad!" her roommate voice exclaimed as she peered over the edge of her bed. Looking straight-faced, she pointed her pencil toward me and said, "Why don't you go to school? They have a college here, and they also have an adult training school. You don't have to work! You can go to school. You can be a full time student! I go to college. There is always room available in the classes."

"School? College?" I joked. Just the thought of school frightens me.

"Don't be silly. I haven't been to school in so long I wouldn't know what to do!" I continued, bracing myself against the door.

"You're never too old to learn!" she sarcastically answered, smiling at me.

"But! But! I have only an 8th grade education. I hate school. I can't do the work," I said.

"Oh! You can do it!" she answered.

"Yes! Miss Dorothy! Why don't you try it? I would much rather see you in school than in the kitchen," Ann scowled at me.

I felt like a deer trapped in a hunter's net.

I looked up at Rudy, Ann's roommate. Her face looked like an angel as she smiled, showing very white teeth. At that moment, a peace came upon me. I hesitated.

"Be a doll and say yes!" Ruby said. I nodded.

"Does that mean yes?" Ann asked as she held out her hands.

"Yes! Yes!" I breathed, and opened the door.

"I'm glad to hear that!" Ruby said.

"Tell me what to do." I asked Ruby.

"In the morning at 8 o'clock, go to the resignation office. Tell the clerk that you want to go to school. Tell her that you are new. She will assist you," she replied.

Back in my room, fear gripped my heart.

"There is no way out," I moaned.

Then I fell on my knees and cried out in a loud voice.

"Father God, nothing can be kept secret from you. You know everything before it happens. Here I am about to go to school. I am afraid. I hate school. I need to do something to gain my good time. If school is what I should do, then when I go in the morning to see about getting in school, give me a sign by letting everything go well for me... And give me favor with the clerk. This I ask in Jesus Name... Amen."

The Lord heard my prayer. The next morning, things went great for me, and that day I was accepted into the education program.

The prison routine was doors popped at 6 o'clock A.M. The doors sounded like guns being fired at a firing range. 6:30 A.M., cottages were called for breakfast separately to the cafeteria. The food was excellent.

8 o'clock A.M., all inmates had to be at their work assignments, except the newcomers.

11 o'clock A.M., inmates were dismissed for lunch. They had to return to their assigned cottages, to be called separately to the cafeteria.

1 o'clock P.M., inmates return to their assigned jobs or school.

4 o'clock P.M., work day ends. Everyone must return to assigned cottages for count. After count, dinner is called by cottages.

After dinner is social time. There were scheduled activities in the gym. There was a track, and ball field. There was a chapel. We had Christian programs nightly, Bible study, church services, musicals, and prayer meetings.

Weekends were off days. Every weekend, there were activities, both Christian and non-Christian. Groups came into the prison to entertain the inmates, such as Ray Charles, Bobby Blue Bland, and James Brown. Many Christian groups came also. Then too, all the well-famous prison ministries came yearly.

Due to the increase in the prison population and the increase in theft, the inmates were not allowed to visit other inmates in their rooms, if they lived in another cottage. However, after being a resident for six months and having many requests for me to pray for inmates, I was given special permission from the Warden to the housing officers of my cottage to allow anyone that needed to come to visit me acceptance.

No matter how hard they strived to survive, no matter how tough or cool they tried to act, whenever I would look into the eyes of the women around me, lights were on, but no one was home! They were all just walking dead women. There was nothing good coming out of their eyes... they were empty. Despair, depression, sadness, hate, bitterness, fear, and loneliness stared back from the faces all around. Many of the ladies were smiling, but smiling faces tells lies. Those smiles were frowns turned upside down. Therefore, I committed to having an open door policy for prayer.

I mailed Billy the form for visiting. The institution had a program for family living unit visits. This consisted of a two nights, three days visit with one's children and husband. The visit could be obtained every six weeks. There was a compound within the facility that had several apartments with a park type playground. This apartment complex had a cyclone fence around it. The apartments was just like homes. The visitor had to bring enough food for three days because once the family came into the complex there was no leaving until the visit ended. Until the time was up, the three days and two nights.

I sent Billy the package, so that he could get himself and the children approved. He filled out the paper work and mailed it back to the counsellor. He and the children were approved. I was very happy. Although I wrote Billy every week, he wouldn't answer my letters.

The day finally arrived for me to take my G.E.D. test. I passed. I then enrolled in the college. The University of La Verne has an onsite college right there on the grounds. The professors from the college would come out every week to teach their classes. The buildings were grouped together on the far North-East side of the prison grounds. The semesters were quarterly.

Despite the fact that I had never been to high school, I was sitting in a college class for the first time in my life, at the age of 42 years old. When I was a teenager I had to work in the cotton fields to help support my family. We were too valuable to go to school. I went to school two months each year, then I was passed to the next grade for the next year until I graduated from the 8th grade.

My first day in college was devastating. I felt I had just crawled from under a rock. I felt so stupid. There were 30 students, all of them were so much younger than I was. They seemed to know so much more than I did. I knew nothing about what the professor was talking about.ss

The other students participated in the lecture, but I was overwhelmed. In my philosophy class, the professor mentioned the name Aristotle. Joy leaped in my heart. I raised my hand, and said, "Onassis!"

"No!" he replied with disgust in his voice.

"One of our philosophies."

Irritated by my lack of knowledge, I concentrated on the hand-out that was given to us at the beginning of the class. I had never seen a syllabus before. The requirement to finish the course gave me goose pimples.

"There is no way I can do this." I thought.

4 o'clock P.M., crossing the crowded compound I hurried to reach my cottage. Walking through the door of my room, I begin to weep. I was deeply disturbed and began to express my fears to God.

I said, "Father God, you, and you alone, spoke the word at the beginning of creation and formed the world. You made me. I look like other people, but I don't feel like other people. I feel so stupid. Why have you allowed me to make a fool of myself? Why did you let me enrol in those college classes? I am so old. How can I compete with a class full of young people? God help me! I don't know what to do! I need your help. Help me! In the name of Jesus help me! Jesus! Jesus!"

I was on my knees crying out to the Lord for a few hours. I didn't want to eat. Then I heard a voice say, "Read, Dorothy!"

When I heard this voice, I fell face downward on the floor, and said to him:

"It would have been better if I had taken a job in the kitchen. I can't understand how to do college work. What can I do?"

The voice answered again.

"Read! Read!"

I felt weak, but I had a sense of peace within my being. I then stood up and walked to my bed sitting on it I took a deep breath, and took my towel in my hand then dabbed away the tears.

Reading became a great escape, as well as a highway out of the darkness of ignorance. I stayed in the library. I took a correspondence bible course from Rhema Bible College in Tulsa, OK. During the next semester at La Verne, I was the most outstanding student. In four semesters I received my A.A. degree. This was a first for the prison. I started with no college credits along with a bleak outlook, but with God's help in 12 months I received my A.A. degree. The college had the graduating ceremony at the main college in La Verne, California. I wasn't allowed to go, but my name was printed in the year book. The University sent my degree to the college administrator of the prison campus.

The administrator of the prison on site University of La Verne College was Mrs. Wright. She wanted to present my degree to me before the class. I agreed.

Next morning, Mrs. Wright came into my class room. The class stopped chattering as she stood in front of the group.

"Good morning;" she said coolly.

"Good morning!" the class responded.

"I am thrilled to present this degree to one of our outstanding students. She has amazed all of us. She enter this program with little hope a year ago. She has now earned her A.A. degree. Dorothy Woods, we are proud of you." Mrs. Wright said as she waved her hands motioning for me to join her in the front of the class. White teeth gleamed as she ushered me, into the spot. I paused to admire intricately worked binder the degree was placed.

Pulses racing, I managed a smile. For a brief moment I surveyed the class all eyes were locked on me.

"Tell us how you did it, Dorothy!" Mrs. Wright asked.

"Thank you, Mrs Wright. First of all, I must give God all the credit. All my life, I thought education was for special people, and I wasn't one of them. But upon enrolling here at La Verne I made a decision, then I made a commitment. Then, I set a goal, and with God's help, I did it!"

11:15 A.M., in my room I praised God. I said:
"I give you thanks, O Lord and King.
I praise you as my God and Savior.
I give you thanks for you have helped me and protected me.
You have rescued me from ignorance, and self-destruction.
You helped me when no one else could.
In your great mercy you saved me.
I thank you for never leaving me.
I will always praise you, and sing hymns of thanksgiving.
You answered my prayer, and saved me from my stupidity.
And so I thank you and praise you,
O Lord, I praise you!"

During the two weeks semester breaks, I had to find part time work, so that I could keep getting gain time. Gain time is good time. I decided to work in the kitchen, washing dishes every semester break. The kitchen was always in need of dish washers. Therefore, I had a standing job always waiting for me. I never had to go job hunting.

One Thursday afternoon, we had to double scrub the kitchen because the assistant superintendent was bringing a group of visitors on a tour.

Two-thirty, they arrived. Mr. Rick, the assistant superintendent and his group, came walking through the cafeteria, very slowly nodding their heads, admiring the super clean facility. They were very polite, speaking to all the workers as they strolled in slow motion. Suddenly, they passed the door of the dish washer room. I stood at attention as if I was in the army.

"Hello!" Mr. Rick said.
"Hello Sir!" I replied.
"How are you today?" Mr. Rick asked.
"I am wonderful, wonderful!" I answered.
Mr. Rick was startled. He stumbled.
"What did you say?" he questioned.
"I said I am wonderful, wonderful!" I answered.
"Wait a minute! How could you be wonderful? It is 100 degrees outside. You're in prison, and you're in this kitchen washing dishes?" he asked abruptly.

I thought quickly, then plumped for the truth.

"Mr. Rick, me being wonderful is not predicated on where I am, or what I am doing. It's because of who I belong to, and where I am going. Mr. Rick, I belong to God. I am a Christian." I replied.

Taking a deep breath, he preceded on with his sight-seeing tour.

Two weeks later, I was walking from the Post Office. The weather was very hot. School had not resumed. However, there was very little movement on the yard because most of the inmates was on their job assignments. I noticed a human figure sprawled under a tree.

"Hey! Hey cutie pie!" the voice screamed from under the shade tree.

I kept walking looking straight ahead. I was not used to hearing such comments, so I refused to look around.

"Foxy lady!" the voice went on…

I moved off rapidly, irritated when she followed me. She kept flirting, until she came within arm's reach.

"Hey cutie!" a lady's voice exclaimed.

Suddenly I turned, and said, "Are you referring to me?"

She stopped dead in her tracks. She begin preaching.

"Oh! Ms. Da'thy, I am so sorry. I didn't see your face. I would never do this to you. Please forgive me. You looked like someone else. I couldn't see that far off. Excuse me! No way would I disrespect you. God forgive me. Please…Please…Please."

"It's okay! I forgive you. Relax!" I replied.

This was the first and only encounter I had with homosexuality during my entire eight years sentence. God will keep you if you want to be kept.

Lord, you have made your people great-glorious in all respects. You have never neglected them. You have given them help, always, everywhere.

Despite knowing that Billy wasn't answering my letters, I continued writing him weekly. I would send him a copy of my semester grades each quarter. Eventually, after the second semester, he decided to let the children come to visit. He let my friend Mary bring them to see me. They came on a Saturday afternoon. The visiting room had a joining room for children. It was like a kindergarten class room. The children was overjoyed. They stayed four hours. There was vending machines. We ate lunch, and played many, many games.

Predictably, the children talked Billy's ears off regarding the splendid time they had when they came to visit me. They wanted a repeat visit the next weekend. Larry came with the children that weekend. Billy refused to bring them. He filled out the visiting forms, but he wouldn't come to see me or come with the children.

To my surprise, Billy sent the children to see me three times by Larry in one month. This was hectic for Larry because this cut into his weekend dates, so I suggested a flu-visit. I sent the forms that listed the dos's and don'ts's of the flu-visit, and also the list of the food allowed on the visits.

As I had expected, the children were extremely excited about coming on a flu-visit. Billy was hesitating, uncertain whether to let the children come. He called my sister Fannie and spoke to her about it. He confided in her that at first he believed that I was crazy, but now he can see that I was not crazy because a crazy person can't go to college and do as well as I was doing.

After their conversation he put his ego in check, and decided to allow the children to come on the flu-visit.

I breathed a sigh of relief when the counsellor called me into her office and told me that Billy had requested a flu-visit for the children. The counsellor had schedule the visit for the last of the month.

Monday morning the day of my flu-visit, I was excused from class because of it. Thrilled with my first flu-visit, I found myself pacing the floor. Murmuring that I hope things go well, the officer came to escort me to the flu-visit apartments. Billy had left the children with the officer at the front gate. All five of them came. We were given a three bedroom apartment. The children was awaiting me in the apartment with an officer.

Excitement quivered through me as we walked to the apartment. The officers then turned and left. The door closed behind them. I stated at the children. They were sitting on the couch. The apartment was homely with two comfortable sofas, two chairs, a coffee table, and two end tables with a floor model television. For the next fifteen minutes the children and I regaled each other with our news. They were excited and amazed to see inside the prison. Tears were pouring down my cheeks when they said, "We can stay here with you! We don't have to go home! We can stay right here!"

We unpacked the luggage, and put the clothing in the bedrooms. Each bedroom had a bedroom set with dressers.

The friendly atmosphere was very noticeable as the children played in the play grounds. There was a kitchen, so I cooked the meals three times a day. In the evening we had bible study, and we all held hands and prayed at the end of the study. I made all the children pray out loud.

"Mommy, you aren't a bad person like my dad and everyone say!" Johnetta exclaimed.

"What do you mean my love?" I asked.

"Well, everybody says you are bad. Daddy says that, too!" she answered.

Not wanting to jeopardise my future visits, I held back the tears. I was disappointed at their father telling them such ridiculous things.

"Come here, everyone. Cut off the TV. Let's talk!" I said.

"Listen, I am not a bad person! I made bad choices. There are no bad people. It's just that people make bad choices. It's the choices that we make that put us in jail or prison. If we make bad choices, we have to pay for them. There are always two choices. One is a bad choice, and one is a good choice. If someone makes a bad choice, she/he will have to pay for it. That goes for everyone. We all must strive to make the right choice in life. Our actions bear fruit. If we make good choices, we won't have to come to a place like this," I preached.

"Yes! Mommy, this place isn't bad," said Jim.

"You are right, but I can't go home with you. I have to stay here a long time. I have to be away from the people I love," I explained.

"There is a lot of people here, too," said Johnetta.

"Yes! But what is the best place in the world to you?" I asked.

"Disneyland!" she answered.

"Would you want to stay there all the time, away from the people you love such as your brothers, sisters, father and mother?" I asked.

"No!" she replied.

"There it is!" I said.

We all held hands, and I prayed for them all.

"O Lord, help us understand that you made everyone good. But it's our choices that are bad. We have to suffer the consequences of our actions. Have mercy on us. In Jesus name I pray, amen."

After a few minutes, Johnetta came with her hands behind her back standing in front of me. She stared me in the face, and said, "Mommy, you explain things so well. I love you."

She then pulled her hands out with a rose in it.

"This is for you. You are a wonderful and pretty as this rose." she stated.

Sensing a need for a hug. I hugged her. She then ran outside, and joined the others on the monkey bars.

CHAPTER 4

The Devil's Work

The children's conversation with me so perturbed me that for the rest of the week I worked at a killing pace, to get a phone call to Billy. I was involved in the Christian ministry, so I did volunteer work to receive phone calls.

During the last flu-visit, Johnetta confined in me regarding the situation that was going on with them at home.

Billy had moved his girlfriend into the house to live with them. She had three teenagers, two boys, and one girl. Her name was Annie. Annie was very mean to them, and her children were also.

One morning, Johnetta walked into her father's bedroom without knocking on the door. He and Annie were having sex. Annie jumped up from the bed, and took Billy's belt from his pants that was on the chair next to the bed.

Annie doubled the belt, and proceed to beat Johnetta profusely.

"You have no manners! I'll teach you some! You want things your way? When I finish with you, you're going to mind me!" Annie screamed as she beat Johnetta down the stairs.

Billy didn't say a word. He acted as if nothing never happened. I was very disturbed. Finally, I was able to reach him on the phone. All sorts of unwanted images flashed before me, and I could happily have boiled him in oil. Nevertheless, I had to be diplomatic because of the children.

"Hello!" he beamed.

"Billy, this is Dorothy," I cried.

"Yes! How are you?" he asked.

"Well, I am wonderful, but I called because I am concerned about the children," I replied.

"What about the children?" he asked.

"You know when we have flu-visits, we all pray. I have taught them how to pray. When they pray, I hear them talking to God about the woman that you have moved into the house," I exploded.

"I need someone to take care of the children. She is my live-in help," he stated.

"Well, the children says she is very mean to them," I said.

"Aren't you over-dramatizing the situation?" he questioned.

Reluctantly, I cut the conversation off.

"I will pray about the situation, and I'll call you back soon," I ended.

In great frustration, I went to my room. I didn't want to jeopardise the children. I needed to handle it with great wisdom. I had to fast and pray. I fasted for three days, and three nights. During the fast, I repeated this Psalms seven times a day aloud:

> "The Lord is my light and my salvation;
> Whom shall I fear? The Lord is the
> strength of my life; of whom shall I be afraid?
> when the wicked, even mine enemies and my
> foes, came upon me to eat up my flesh, they
> stumbled and fell.
> Though a host should encamp against
> me, my heart shall not fear:
> though war should rise against me,
> in this will I be confident.
> One thing have I desired of the
> Lord, that will I seek after; that I
> may dwell in the house of the Lord
> all the days of my life, to behold the
> beauty of the Lord, and to inquire in
> his temple.
> For in the time of trouble he shall
> hide me in his pavilion; in the
> secret of his tabernacle shall he hide me;
> he shall set me up upon a rock.
> And now shall mine head be lifted
> up above mine enemies round about me;
> therefore will I offer in his tabernacle
> sacrifices of joy; I will sing, yea, I will
> sing praises unto the Lord.
> Hear, o Lord, when I cry with my voice;
> have mercy also upon me, and answer me.

When thou saidst, seek ye my face;
my heart said unto thee, thy face,
Lord, will I seek.
Hide not thy face far from me;
put not thy servant away in anger:
thou hast been my help; leave me not,
neither forsake me, O God of my salvation.
When my father and my mother forsake me,
then the Lord will take me up.
Teach me thy way, O Lord, and
lead me in a plain path, because of
mine enemies.
Deliver me not over unto the will of
mine enemies; for false witnesses, are
risen up against me, and such as
breathe out cruelty.
I have fainted unless I had believed
to see the goodness of the Lord
in the land of the living.
Wait on the Lord; be of good
courage, and he shall strengthen
thine heart; wait I say, on the Lord.
Psalms 27"

Love had me blinded. I had mixed emotions about calling Billy. I felt an extremely urged on the inside to take a stand, and get Annie out of that house.

The next day, I went to the chaplain to request a phone call. He granted it to me. Dialling his number seemed very hard to me.

"Don't be scared," I kept repeating over and over as I dialled.

"Hello Billy," I said.

"Yes!" he murmured.

"Well, I told you I would call you back after I had prayed about the situation regarding the kids," I confessed.

"What's worrying you?" he demanded.

For an instant I hesitated, then decided to be frank. He might be the father of the children, but I refused to regard him as an ogre out to destroy me. I'll stand up for the rights of those children even if I lose him. This action might put Billy even further out of my orbit, not that he had ever been in it. I reminded myself, he was a star in a galaxy of his own.

Irritated by my fanciful notions, I concentrated on the conversation.

"I have decided that you must make Annie move."

"Move?" he cut in.

"Yes! She must! She is no good for the children," I said.

"I will not let you control my house from prison!" he exploded.

"I tell you that if you don't have her out of there within 30 days, I am going to call the lawyers. She absolutely must go! I insist," I assured him.

"You are doing this for selfish reasons," he stated.

"Call it what you must!" I said.

"She will not be moving!" He said as he hung the phone up with a bang in my ear. I was furious.

Four-thirty found me in my room on my knees again praying:

"Father God, give me your forgiving spirit. Take this bitterness, this desire for revenge, this grudge, this hatred, out of me. In Jesus name, I pray."

Irritated and on edge, I spent the evening writing Billy a 12 page letter. Quite unnecessary, I knew, but it kept me occupied. The next morning, I dressed with great care: my tried, and trusted means of keeping up my spirits, and I set off to my college classes.

Predictably, Annie and her children moved out within 30 days. They moved to Altadena, California, the next town adjoining Pasadena. Annie's two teenage boys were gang members, they were part of the "Bloods", there was a rival gang called "Crips". During the months Annie was living in the house with Billy, the Crips were looking for Annie's two sons. These two boys had a bounty on their heads because of a drug deal gone badly. Two weeks after Annie moved to Altadena; a Molotov cocktail was thrown into her house while they were all asleep: about 4:30 A.M. in the wee hours of the morning. The house became a towering inferno. The two boys were burned to death. Annie suffered from third degree burns, and died in the hospital weeks later.

Her daughter survived from minor burns. Upon hearing the news from Larry, my son, I wept profusely. For Annie first: then for me, following the inward witness that compelled me to take action. If I had disobeyed, that tragedy would have happened to my children.

Regrettably, I received my first letter from Billy. He said that he had seen a lawyer about getting a divorce. I refuse to consider such a thing. I sat in deep mourning. I was terrified.

Angrily pushing aside the thought of him divorcing me; I went to bed. I couldn't sleep: I tried counting sheep: Sleep wouldn't come.

Miserably I pushed aside the single blanket covering me, and I sat up in bed looking through the window. Unlike in Pasadena, there were few lights visible at this ungodly hour, and the glimmer of light from the gun tower did little to alleviate my unhappy mood. But as I sat there, shivering slightly in the cool air of night, my fighting spirit revived. I was damned if I would allow Billy to intimidate me. If the worst came to the worst I would have given him my best effort.

Laying all pride aside I wrote him a letter begging him please don't divorce me. I explained to him that it was inappropriate at this time. I apologized for the Annie incident. I assured him that I loved him, and I wanted to be with him to raise our children together. Not getting a reply from him; I assumed that meant he wouldn't divorce me.

Three weeks later the children came on another flu-visit. Billy dropped them off at the gate on Monday and he came to pick them up at the end of the visit. I was so full of joy and wonder that I was about to explode.

Finally, I received a card from Billy telling me that he was coming to visit me. He gave me the date that he was coming. With great joy and gladness I sang all night.

Anxious to be at my best for my first visit with Billy I avoided meats and sugar.

Due to us having to program during the day; visiting didn't start on the week day until 4 o'clock P.M.

6:30 P.M., I was still waiting for my name to be called for my visit. I was so beset by nerves I sat still. I paced the floor after waiting for three hours. When the telephone rang for my visit it was 30 minutes before closing the visiting room. I ran.

"What could have gone wrong? Why so late? Maybe he had car trouble," the thoughts kept coming in my mind as I ran to the visiting room.

I refused to think beyond this point, aware that my marriage depended on the outcome. I acknowledged, though as I walked in the door that I wished this visit had occurred when I was in a more relaxed frame of mind. Fat chance! When I was near Billy, I was tense as an overwound spring.

As I entered the visiting room I saw Billy standing on the patio near the second set of tables. I checked in at the reception desk. I then rush to Billy; impulsively I kissed his lips. He flushed and I instantly apologised.

"What happened?" I asked.

"What do you mean? He demanded.

"Well, you are so late!" I replied.

His face was expressionless.

"I'm not late. I have enough time," reaching in his pocket, he pulls out some white papers. "I want you to sign the property over to me. I have the papers here for you to sign. I am getting a divorce," he explained.

For an instant, I hesitated. Speechless with shock, I held the papers. As I took them from his hands, he jerked back as though I had hit him.

"I can't sign this. I begged you to stop the divorce. I figured you had. I thought this was a visit so you could talk about our future plans," I exploded.

"Why do you enjoy deliberately misunderstanding me, Dorothy?" he corrected.

"Why do you want a divorce?" I asked.

"I don't have any choice! I'm in a tricky situation, and I can't let my personal feeling sway me!" he confessed.

Mystified as to the reason for the visit, it had irritated me to the screaming point.

"I will not sign these papers. I will never sign them!" I told him.

Dumbly, I stared at him as he walked out of the visiting room.

I nodded regretting I couldn't have given my heart to a Christian man, God-fearing man, instead of a man who didn't understand the meaning of the word love.

Nine-thirty found me in my room again faced down in agony crying aloud to God. The next day, angrily pushing aside the thought of Billy, I escaped in my school work.

Ten days later, I received a letter from classification stating that the institution had started a pilot program for the Fire Department. This program would train inmates on how to fight fires, and I had been enlisted into the program. My immediate reaction was that of disbelief. It couldn't be! Life wasn't so cruel. Yet it was, and not just cruel, but diabolical, for I had been enlisted.

The next morning, I took the letter to the college administrator. She called the classification committee to let them know that I was in school, and I was doing great in my classes. Also, she wanted me to continue my college work. Her plea fell on deaf ears.

I filed a 602. The 602 is an inmate complaint form. My complaint was denied. I then, wrote a letter to the superintendent of the prison. Her response was that she couldn't interfere with the functions of the classification committee. Disconcerted, I frowned.

"So it is!"

Trouble is, I went on, to the assignment because I didn't want to lose any good-time/work-time. To add insult to injury I had to do exercises six hours a day without ever seeing a physician. We were all enlisted without a physical examination.

Devastated, I appealed my 602 requesting to have a hearing. The hearing was granted. I programed in the morning; and stayed home that afternoon waiting to be called for my hearing.

At 2:10 P.M., I was called. The weather was extremely hot, and the inmates was trying to find a cool breeze. It wasn't easy walking for the pavement was a sea of bodies moving like a sluggish tide. Yet everyone was good-tempered despite the heat and noise.

I walked in the office at the A.D.M. building. The reception asked me to have a seat as she failed to announce my arrival.

A.D.M. was as modern inside as out, with teak desks, black leather chairs, and a proliferation of flowering plants.

Giving my name to the committee member, Mr. Henry, I was escorted to a huge air-conditioned room. There was a long table with three other people seated. Two women on the left, and a grey headed man on the right side of the table.

Mr. Henry walked to the front end of the table; I followed behind to a chair on the right of him; on the side of the table. Silently he sat down, motioning me to do the same, and he took a straight-back chair in front of the table.

"Mrs. Woods, you are here to address the committee regarding the Fire Camp issue. This is the committee. On my left, Mrs. Smith, and Mrs. Green; on my right, Mr. Hall," Mr. Henry drawled.

"Good afternoon!" I nodded.

Each member had a copy of my records before them. Mr. Henry was thumbing through his files. After a few minutes, he started.

"It's regrettable, you don't like our program. I'm a pragmatist, Mrs. Woods, and I don't cut off my nose to spite my face. I chose you because you are outstanding in the way you program in this institution, and we see you on the track all the time. You jog every day!" Mr. Henry said.

"Mr. Henry, age makes no difference to you?" I asked.

Leaping up from his chair as if he was going to run out of the room he screamed.

"A.I.D.S.?"

"No. Age," I corrected him.

Restraining himself, he sat back in his chair, and leaned back with a sigh of relief.

"No, age makes no different to us," he thundered.

"So I am being punished for being a model prisoner?" I confessed.

"Mrs. Woods, you belong to the state. We represent the state, and you do what we tell you to do! You have no say so," said a voice in front of me; it was Mrs. Green. I looked into her eyes, and they were turning red as a beet by the minute. She went on.

"You have come here, and within 12 months you got your A.A. Degree. What more do you want from us? No one has ever done that. Now you owe us!"

"I want to get my B.A." I stated.

"Well, you're not going to get it here. Get it when you get out of here!" she yelled.

"You are going to Fire Camp, and that's it," said Mrs. Smith.

"I can see this committee has made up its mind," I said.

"You're right!" said Mr. Hall.

Raising from my chair, I said, "Well, thank you for your time. Have a good day!"

There was silence, and from the corner of my eye, I saw Mr. Henry standing stiff as a ramrod, as if awaiting an explosion. But I was relaxed, and the ladies just sat in their chairs looking surprised. Mr. Hall was rubbing his hands, and nodding his head as I exited the room.

Afterwards I took a stroll, upbraiding myself for being nervous. I met Cathy; she was taking a break from her computer class.

"Did you go to classification today?" she asked.

"Yes, I did." I replied.

"Was they helpful? Are you going back to school?" she questioned.

"Regrettably not." I answered.

Astounded, she abruptly turned to walk back to her class because her break was over.

"Let's have dinner together tonight!" I said.

"Right! I'll see you then!" she responded.

Back in my room, again despondency swamped me; and with an effort I shook it off. I had to think of a new plan. I had exalted all avenues inside the prison system, so I must go outside of the prison for help. Yet, I wasn't going to fail, and it was negative to think otherwise. Where there is a will, there has to be a way. There is always more than one way to skin a cat.

Resolutely, I concentrated on what to do next. Billy was outside. He was my outside connection, but to get him to help me was like a castrated man trying to rape a young woman.

The call came for my cottage to go to dinner. I was so beset by nerves I could only toy with dinner. Cathy and I talked. She wanted to help.

"Are you all right?" she asked.
"Yes!" I answered.
"Well, have you come up with a solution to your problem?" she asked.
"In part, yes!" I replied.
I was pushing my food round in my plate when I had a flash.
"Cathy, I know what to do, but I will need a lot of help from you. I mean, not just in here. On the outside, too!" I confessed.
"Sure I'll help you!" she assured me.
"Well, this is the plan: I am going to the library to get the addresses of all the politicians of California. Tonight, we will compose a letter to them. Tomorrow you will use the computer, and write them all the same letter including the governor. Then, we will send a box of excess clothing and books to your daughter. In the box, we will camouflage the letters. Then have your daughter mail them for me, because they will not let the letters go out from here," I explained.
"Good heavens! You have really been thinking. You should run for a political office. My, what a brain! Yes! Absolutely! Let's go!" she stated.

Ten days later the calls started coming into the institution regarding my accusation. We sent out 25 letters, and most all of them responded. I became the talk of the institution.

Eventuality, I was summoned to the A.D.M. building again to see the classification committee. Angrily, they met with me. Mr. Henry came out in the hall to escort me to the conference table. Diplomatically silent, I followed him into the room where the other members were awaiting me. They were proud people, and disliked losing face.

"Mrs. Woods, you got the nerves. Writing the governor. We have so many phone calls coming in regarding you," Mr. Henry said.
"How did you get the letters out of the institution?" Mr. Hall asked.
"No comment!" I frowned.
"Well you can go back to school," said Mrs. Smith.
"Permanently?" I asked.
"Yes!" she said.
"Thank you very much!" I said.

Entering the college classes for the second time; I found it even more welcoming than on the first occasion, and I was sorry I hadn't thought to go to college long ago. Talk about anti-climax! I entered the classroom and dissolved into tears. I had never expected to get back in the classes before the quarter was over. I had a lot of making up to do to catch up in my homework.

A few days later, I received the divorce papers from Billy's attorney. Agitatedly I paced the floor. The urge to talk it out impelled me to go to the Chaplain. I walked to his office. He sat and listened as I talked.

Hearing myself speak lent strength to my assertion that Billy was a gold digger, and only then did I relax.

CHAPTER 5

Answered Prayer

During that time I started spending a lot of time in prayer. I learned to do spiritual warfare. I would confess daily:

I am now releasing my faith by confessing this is the greatest day of my life. This is the day that the Lord has made, and has allowed me to see it (when I say day, I don't mean as in one day, but I mean a period of time, such as when one says, "In my grandmother's day or the day of the covered wagon"). I will rejoice and be glad in it. I am free from the curse of the law. Jesus became a curse for me. Christ has redeemed me from the curse of the law, being made a curse for me, for it is written; "Cursed is every one that hangeth on a tree." Galatians 3:13

Therefore, sin, sickness, worry, soudt, fear, poverty, and all that Satan represents shall have no power over me. I have been redeemed.

I cover myself with the blood of Jesus Christ and claim that protection of His blood for my family, my finances, my home, my spirit, my soul, and my body. I surrender myself completely in every area of my life to you, Jesus.

I take a stand against all the workings of the Devil that would try to hinder me from best serving you.

I address myself only to the true and living God, and refuse any involvement of Satan in my prayer life.

Satan, I command you, and all of your demon forces of darkness, in the name of Jesus Christ to leave my presence. I bring the blood of Jesus Christ between you, my family, my home, my finances, my spirit, my soul, and my body. I declare, therefore, Satan that you, and your wicked spirits are subject to me, in the name of the Lord Jesus Christ.

Furthermore, in my own life today I destroy and tear down all of the strongholds of the enemy and smash every plan that has been formed against me and my family. I tear down the strongholds of the Devil against my mind, and I surrender my mind to you, blessed Holy

Spirit. I affirm, Heavenly Father, that you have not given me the spirit of fear, but of power, and of love, and of a sound mind. Therefore, I resist the spirit of fear in the name of Jesus, the son of the living God, and I refuse to fear, refuse to doubt, refuse to worry, because I have authority over all the power of the enemy, and nothing shall by any means hurt me. I claim complete and absolute victory over the forces of darkness in the Name of Jesus Christ, and I bind the Devil and command him to get out of my life. He cannot stay. Every mountain of Satanic adversity in my life must go this very moment, and by faith I call it done.

I break and smash the strongholds of Satan formed against my emotions today, and I give my emotions to you dear God. I destroy the strongholds of Satan against my will today. I give my will to you, Heavenly Father, and choose to make the right decisions of faith. I breakdown the strongholds of Satan against my body today, and I give my body to you God, realizing that I am the temple of the Holy Ghost.

Again, I cover myself with the blood of the Lord Jesus Christ, and pray that the Holy Ghost would bring all the work of the crucifixion, all the work of the resurrection, all the work of the ascension of the Lord Jesus Christ into my life today. I surrender my life and possessions to you dear God. I refuse to fear, worry, or be discouraged, in the name of Jesus.

I will not hate, envy, or show any type of bitterness towards my brothers, sisters, or my enemies; but I will love them with the love of God shed abroad in my heart by the Holy Ghost.

Open my eyes and show me the areas of my life that do not please you, and give me the strength, grace, and wisdom to remove any sin or weight that would prevent our close fellowship. Work in me to cleanse me from all ground that would give the devil a foothold in my life. I, claim, in every way the victory of the cross over all satanic forces in my life. By faith, in faith, through faith, and with faith, I pray, in Jesus Name.

Six months before my release, I submitted my plans to the parole board. I prayed for a ride home, a good church that I could be affiliated with, and a home to go to.

My prayers were answered. My son Larry had a one bedroom apartment that he and my daughter Lesa resided in. I planned to stay with him for a period of three weeks until I could get my own apartment per our agreement, which I would later regret.

Refuge Christian Center in Altadena had responded to my letter of fellowship needs. The pastor assured me that I was welcome into their congregation. I would receive the right hand of fellowship, and be accepted as any other member of the congregation.

Over my period of incarceration, I had because close and best friends with Betty. Her husband knew of me through our fellowship over the past years. Upon the news of my release, Betty arranged with her husband to pick my daughter, Lesa, up in San Gabriel and escort her to come and pick me up. As my release date drew closer, I became more excited. Like New Year's Eve countdown only better. My fellow Christian inmates shared my excitement and enthusiasm.

June 26, 1986: my release date. The joy, pure ecstasy. I had gone past the state of happiness. The state of bliss. All around me were my close friends. Wishing me well. Giving me their blessings. Helping pamper me for my journey home.

All of us walked to the gate together. Gathering in a circle of love, a love circle for our last prayer together in the presence of the Lord. Holding hands, we all prayed, for me, for each other. The tears of joy flowed.

"Now, all this pampering you've done to me, the tears have messed me up," I said.

We said our final good-byes. I walked to the release center. My final search of meager personal items. I sat on a long wooden bench waiting for my ride. Fifteen minutes. Thirty minutes. Forty-five minutes. An hour had passed.

"A limo is coming, a limo is coming here!" the officer shouted with excitement.

Sitting on the bench, I beamed. "That's my ride! Thank you Jesus!" bursting inside with joy, I smiled.

The limo stops in front of the office out in the yard. A very distinguished uniformed driver steps out of the limo, proceeds to the right rear passenger door. Holding my breath in excitement, the handsome uniformed man assists my daughter, Lesa, from the limo, taking her hand.

Watching Lesa step out of the limo, she was gorgeous. Stepping out of vogue, right off the page. Her hair immaculate. Her clothes beautifully tailored. Lesa walks into the reception area, walks to the counter. All the polish and class illuminated the area. Setting on the bench, my heart swelled with pride, joy, and love. The admiration I felt for her was indescribable. Taking note of my surroundings, the female officers were in awe, dumbstruck, but very willing to help her.

"I'm here to pick up Dorothy Woods!" said Lesa from the counter.

Standing, I walked towards Lesa. Her arms outstretched we hugged.

"I thought this day would never come!" Lesa said to me.

"It didn't seem like it! You're an hour late!" I replied.

We both laughed as we were walking arm in arm out the door. Some of the inmates saw me from behind the fence. They began waving and yelling their best wishes, jumping up and down in my excitement I returned their waves.

"Thank you Jesus! Free at last! I'm free at last!" I screamed.

The driver held open our door as we sank into the luxury of the limo. Cold beverage were awaiting us. The view seemed so much more alive. The leaves, the trees, everything. Life was coursing through everything.

We cruised the 60 freeway to the 10 freeway then to the 210. I drank everything, admiring the scenery.

We arrived at Larry's house. He was at work.

I called my friend from church who had arranged a dinner party celebration. Eve picked me up at about 2:30 p.m. We awaited the arrival of the fellow church members who were invited.

The part was wonderful. I met my church member's friends, many for the first time. I was greeted and accepted with open arms.

Eve had really out done herself. She had prepared all my favorite food: fried chicken, smothered cabbage, corn bread, fried okra, pound cake, and peach cobbler. Lots of cold iced tea to quench our thirst.

Larry joined the party just after 5:10 P.M. and at 8:30 P.M. we had had our fill of food. The three of us went home to start our life anew. Thank you Jesus!

> "Therefore if any man be in Christ, he is a new creature, old things are passed away: behold, all things are become new."
> **2 Corinthian 5:17**

CHAPTER 6

Picking Up The Pieces

Living with my son, Larry, was an answer to my prayers. After my release from C.I.W., I took up short term residence in San Gabriel on Rosemead Blvd. My daughter, Lesa, was preparing to leave the one bedroom apartment she shared with Larry, her older brother, heading for college.

I didn't plan on spending much of my time at home. I had enrolled and been accepted as a full-time student at Cal-State Los Angeles. My goal was to complete my college education; Bachelor of Science in Sociology. I received student loans and grants to further my education and enabling me at 44 years old to do so.

With my daughter in an out of state college, and until I could find reasonable housing I would reside with my older son, Larry. Culture shock was sitting in. In looking for a simple and modest apartment I hit so many brick walls. In the short time frame of less than five years, apartment prices had more than doubled.

Prior to my incarceration a one bedroom apartment rented for about $200.00 a month. Four years seven months later, they rent for $450.00 a month. Inflation was out of control. I was very appreciative of my son's generosity. When applying for residency at several locations, had things really changed that much, or had I?

At least for the time being, I could stay with Larry. Praise God! Within a week of Lesa leaving San Gabriel to attend the University of Southern Illinois, my son, Louis, came to California from Colorado Springs, Colorado to live with us.

Three of us in a one bedroom apartment. We did things in shifts. Eating. Our coming and going from the apartment. All three of us had full-time commitments. Louis was a newly registered full-time student at Temple City High School. I was a full-time student in college. And Larry was the only means of support, full-time. Since

Lesa had moved out and Louis, a minor and full-time student with a mother that was unemployed and a full-time college student, he was eligible to receive welfare-benefits just as Lesa had received.

The two small bi-monthly checks, $153.00 each, helped ease the tremendous financial burden from Larry. Our daily routines fell into place. The only glitch was the apartment manager. Larry's lease was for a single individual, although the management would allow two people in a one bedroom apartment. Our arrangements exceeded that by one person. Our dilemma was, who was going to move. Louis was a minor, although junior in high school was capable of living with either Larry or myself. Being a full-time college student, my funds were limited to my student loans and grants for school, not necessarily living expenses such as apartment rent.

That following Saturday, the apartment manager confronted Larry with an ultimatum: one person would have to vacate the premises or everyone would be evicted from the apartment. Tempers flared. Larry was furious for being put in this position, having always been a good tenant, paying his rent on time. Larry lashed out at me, he felt I was dragging my feet, not being sympathetic to his situation with the substantial increase in housing and the general cost of living. He was angry that Louis had moved in, although Larry invited him to stay with us. It appeared that when things didn't go well, he blamed me. I had intruded his apartment; taking over his home.

As our angry words flew back and forth, Louis tried to officiate this sparring match. We were family and shouldn't be at each other's throats. We should support each other no matter what. Larry was concerned about his reputation with the manager and his friends; he was beyond reason. Making no head way towards a truce, I finally suggested that I move out.

Louis could remain with Larry. Why should he suffer any upset? That same day I called a friend from church. I stayed the weekend with her and her son. After I explained the tough spot I was in, we looked for a room for me to rent. That weekend I called referrals from acquaintances at church had given me. I found a man that had a two bedroom house. He occupied one room and he rented the second room to me. That Tuesday, I gathered my meager belongings and moved into Mr. English's residence.

Rethinking my plan of actions I felt that Louis could stay with Larry until I had large enough apartment to accommodate both Louis and I. I would have to seek employment to keep with the additional costs.

I knew Louis was being taken care of by Larry. He received financial assistance to cover his living expenses. I didn't notify the case worker concerning my change in residence. It was an emergency change on my behalf, not a change for Louis. I felt I had nothing to worry about. My one bedroom rental in Mr. English's house was a temporary move, approximately sixty days.

"Trail 'em, nail 'em, and jail 'em!" was the slogan the probation department had in the 80's. I had been trailed since my date of parole. The Welfare Department was contacted via the Parole Department, inquiring if I had notified them of my move from my son's apartment.

Having never notified the Welfare Caseworker of my move, the Caseworker made a home call in person to Larry's apartment. Speaking with Larry, he confirmed what the Parole Officer had reported. Immediately, the Caseworker notified the Parole Officer that I had committed "Welfare Fraud"; I had abandoned my 15 year old son.

I couldn't move back in with Larry, so Louis and I moved to Los Angeles into my sister's home. Even though we were residing in the same residence, the Caseworker still was not satisfied. I contacted Legal Aid concerning the allegations of Welfare Fraud, notified them of what had occurred and the situation had been rectified. However, the Welfare Department filled their claim to the Parole Department. In turn, the Parole Department came back to see me anymore, saying it's a bad environment for the children.

"I sure won't go myself... I don't want no crazy woman!" was Billy's excuse.

My heart was crushed again. I once again cried out to the Lord.

"Why! Why me? Why is this happening to me?"

I felt rejected, abandoned, abused, misused, and manipulated. All of these negative emotions surfaced. I was spiritually depressed, but I kept calling out to the Lord. Here I was doing His good works, but I was being persecuted.

Laying in my bed, I was troubled, and disturbed as I thought about what Billy was doing.

I began to express my fears to God. I said.

"Lord! Why is this happening to me?"

I listened. I listened waiting for a sign or something. Then I prayed.

"Father God, you see, I'm helping these women in here. They are dealing with the worst thing that could happen to them, the loss of their freedom, and I minister to them every day. Many women have given their hearts to you, Lord, for the first time in their lives. I can only see a good father. And yet so many people around me, including Billy, see badly. Help me, Lord! "

I cried and I cried. I cried until I had no more tears. I was drained. Then about midnight I saw a vision of God. I heard the Lord speak to me, and I felt His power. Looking up from my bed, exhausted from crying, I saw a light. The light shone like polished brass. It was so bright I couldn't keep my eyes open.

I heard my name twice.

"Dorothy, Dorothy."

I felt my body raising into a sitting position, all so effortlessly. My feet touching the floor. The voice went on to say, "I have seen your tears. I'm here with you. I'll never leave you or forsake you. I love you."

And with that, I fell soundly asleep, knowing that even in the worst situation, my solid faith in his plans for me will come to fruition.

The next day I was called for another court hearing due to the recent unannounced move. The issue was brought up by my Parole officer, and has recounted all evidence against me. I tried my best to support my claim and reason with the court, but despite that, their decision still violated me, and subsequently I was arrested, and charged with Welfare Fraud.

I had been honest. I told them what happened. I wasn't covering anything up. How could I abandoned my 15 year old son? He was living with my adult son with my permission.

I complied with the terms and conditions of my parole. The receptionist greeted me warmly as I entered the lobby of the Alhambra Parole Office. I was right on time for my scheduled meeting with Mr. Green, my parole officer. Setting in the lobby I completed my monthly report, returning it to the receptionist. I could hear the intercom announcing my availability.

"Mr. Green, Mrs. Woods is ready to see you."

Waiting was painstaking. Finally the door opened. Mr Green greeted me with his usual enthusiasm. I walked just ahead of him. As I was familiar with the office layout, this was my tenth month with Mr. Green. I entered his office with him in back. Before I could seat myself in one of the chairs across from his desk, he said.

"Dorothy Woods, you're under arrest."

"Under arrest?"

"What for?"

"Welfare Fraud. The Welfare Department said you admitted to abandoning your son."

"I explained to them what happened!"

"I'm sorry! There is nothing I can do. I have orders from higher ups. Turn around and put your hands behind your back!"

Standing in a daze, I thought…

"I'm just getting my life together. College. What about school? How could this be? I must be dreaming. I hadn't done anything. Surely they can't think that this is welfare fraud! I was trying to get my children back together."

Turning around, I placed my hands behind my back. The coolness of the stainless steel bracelets, handcuffs… I began to cry and yell, not for me, but for my children.

"I can't believe this. I didn't do nothing!"

My head fell forward, my chin resting on my chest. Mr. Green led me to the back door of the office to the parking lot. All the way to his car, I wept. Tears falling down my face. Settling in the back seat of his car, he drove me to the county jail for booking.

It was a catch 22. Being caught up in the system is all about plea bargaining. Plea bargains is pleading guilty to the charges with the prosecuting attorney giving you a lesser offense and time. If I had not plead guilty, and plea bargained I was facing five years in prison for not notifying the welfare of my address change. Deciding to cut my losses I plea bargained for ten months incarceration, and five years' probation, which was the exact amount of time I had been on parole without incident.

Anyone paroled has an automatic three years of supervised release, meaning, completing a monthly report of activities, and provided to Parole Officer. However, after 12 months of release without any violations, or contact with law enforcement or additional charges, and complying with your Parole Officer, you are automatically released from supervision. I only had two months to go.

CHAPTER 7

Entrapment

> "And the multitude crying aloud began to desire him to do as he had ever done unto them. (v8) But Pilate answered them, saying, will ye that I release unto you the King of the Jesus?" (v9)

I was a Christian, and this was happening to me. I had no intention of defrauding the Welfare Department. I attended church every Sunday, never missing a Sunday for ten months. I was working in the church faithfully. My pastor had baptized me. I was obedient to God, living a Godly life in every aspect.

Many men wanted to date me, and have me live with them as a girlfriend, but I never let them touch me sexually. The Lord took care of me, and I didn't bring disgrace to the name of the Lord.

After my arrest, I was so embarrassed and ashamed that I sighed and began to cry. Then, as I choked back my tears, I prayed:

> "Father God, you are righteous.
> You are merciful in all you do,
> faithful in all Your ways.
> You are the judge of this world
> I beg You, treat me with kindness
> You know what happened about the Welfare
> You see what they are doing to me.
> O' Lord, there is no difference for you
> between helping the mighty, and helping the weak.
> Help me O' Lord, my God, for I rely on you. Amen. Amen!"

I called the Caseworker at the Welfare Department. She informed me that the Department was upset with me for putting Louis on welfare, after I had made them look like a "fool" to the world. She went on to tell me that the Department had had a meeting about me, and it was said in this meeting that, "She has plenty of guts if she come back to the same town, and apply for AFDC again."

I also learned that my picture was given to all the workers, and the Department had wedge an all-out war against Dorothy Woods.

I went back to my cell and shouted to my roommate.

"They have tricked me!"

"Who?" She asked.

"The Welfare Department!" I said.

I sat on my bed, wild cries and shouts were heard from my cell.

Some of the inmates I came in contact with while this time of incarceration at S.B.I. were people I had met before. Many of them were also back for violation. They were surprised I was back too.

S.B.I. had changed in many ways. The facility was vastly overcrowded. In 1981-82, 800 women were housed in the jail. Returning in 1987 there were 2,000 females. Everyone was doubled bunked. The food had drastically changed to the worse, with less portions. The building was dirty. There was rats in the rooms.

The staff of officers had become more emotionally and physically brutal. We were herded like cattle, not humans. Due to the increased number of inmates, I was less a concern to the staff when it came to my organizing bible studies, and prayer meetings.

I started my ministry work again. Over the following months, I witnesses more lives changing. God was definitely alive and real. I was able to lead more women to the Lord, than in the previous years of my incarceration.

The inmates were shocked as to the reason why I had been violated.

"I know many people whose kids are with their grandparents, or other members of their family, and the mother receives the welfare check," many ladies would say to me. Then, too, some would say, "Why is God letting this happen to you?"

But many others would confess.

"I can't believe God is letting this happen. It's plain to see that the Welfare Department hates you!"

I was so angry. I had an all-out war on the devil. I knew God was sovereign. God had allowed men to do this to me. I was determined that anyone I met who didn't know the Lord, I would lead them to Him. I knew the devil wouldn't like that. I started campaigning. I'd lead people to God in groups. This helped me to deal with the injustice that was going on in my life.

I taught the people how to cultivate a relationship with God. If we want an exciting life in Christ, and God's plan to come alive in our lives, then we have to do our part.

There is a Godward side, and a man ward side in developing a closer relationship with God. Becoming strong and healthy in the Lord is much the same as working out in an exercise class. Salvation is a free gift. But the development of Spiritual Muscles comes from working out. No one can do this for you.

The exciting friendship that made the difference between religion, and knowing God personally would take work, time, and dedication. Therefore, I treated the Christian fellowship group like we were in Boot Camp.

I trained them how to maintain this relationship with God. I've had to spend time with God like we do in building an ordinary friendship.

In a normal relationship we spend time, talking, working, playing, and doing things together. The same is true in knowing God. We must spend time with Him.

Praying is talking with God. We came together for prayer three times a day. Then we would spend time praising God after the prayer meetings. We would praise Him for such things as our health, friends, talents, hope, salvation, Jesus, and the word of God.

Twice a day, we would met and read the bible. Reading the bible is important in developing a relationship with God, because the bible is the word of God. God and His word are one. Therefore, as we read the bible, God will start speaking to us through the Holy Spirit, who resides in our heart.

One talks to God in prayer. God speaks to one through His word, the bible. It becomes a two-way conversation. The more time spent with the Lord in prayer, and bible study the more intimate and real personal relationship with God becomes.

Fellowship and worship are next, like anything else, hang out with others who are of a similar mind and purpose, Grow and share in the Lord Jesus Christ with other Christians. The old saying, "Birds of a father, flock together" is true in the Christian family. The family of God is one of the great blessings of the Christian world.

Sometimes it isn't easy to see how God is working through people, situations, and even ourselves. That is the reason I was astounded that members of the church congregation that I fellowshipped with believed the newspapers and television reports. They judged me according to the media, not by what the bible says. To them the news media had more validity than the bible. That caused me such hurt and pain. During my time of incarceration I had very little support, mail or visits from any of the members of my church.

In the meantime, Louis was back with Larry, but not receiving any support from the Welfare Department. Times was extremely hard for Larry. Louis found himself a part-time job after school to make ends meet.

Not only was I incarcerated, I also lost a year of college; it put me behind. The system victimized me. The process of rehabilitation was a struggle all the way, no support in any manner. I found my attitude toward the establishment becoming bitter. I was being punished not rehabilitated.

> "Behold I go forward, but he is not there, and backward, but I cannot perceived him: on the left hand, where he doth work, but I cannot behold him; he hideth himself on the right hand, that I cannot see him. But he knoweth the way that I take: when he hath tried me, I shall come forth as gold."
> **Job 28:8-10**

Being a Christian in jail, and being alive for the Lord and wanting to do things God's way doesn't mean that I didn't have problems. Billy was divorced from me. He was now incarcerated in the state prison. He had applied for the half-way house in Los Angeles. However, now that I was back in jail the system denied his application to go to the half-way house. Billy was angry with me, because of this. But the Lord had made Himself so real to me, that I looked for the good in all things, and in all people.

I could let go of the past bad experiences with Billy. It was not that big of a burden anymore, because God was doing it with me.

> "And Jesus came and spoke unto them. Saying, All power is given unto me in heaven and in earth. Go ye therefore, and teach all nations baptizing them in the name of the Father, and of the Son, and of the Holy Ghost. Teaching them to observe all things whatsoever I have commanded you: and, so, I am with you always, even unto the end of the world, Amen." **Matthew 28:18-20.**

Billy's attorney came to the jail to see me. He wanted to talk about a divorce settlement in regards to the real estate that was left unsettled. I agreed that we could settled the matter. He then told Billy that I had no hard feelings, and that I would be willing to go along with his request. This agreement had nothing to do with the children. The issue with the children was already settled with another court, and another attorney. In deep mourning, I fasted all that day the Holy Spirit kept reminding me of what David said in Psalm 37:

> "Fret not thyself because of evil doers, neither be thou envious against the workers of iniquity." (v1)

That day I begin to let go and let God handle the situation. God hears our voices. He hears every voice. There are no prison walls so high or thick, surrounded by enough razor wire, attack dogs and machine gun guards to keep the love of Jesus out. Jesus is real in my life. He answered my prayers. He came into my heart. He walks with me daily, where ever I am God is there too. I can be no place that God is not.

CHAPTER 8

Starting Over Again

February 7, 1988. I was released from S.B.I. after ten months of incarceration. My immediate plans were to temporarily stay with a female member of my church. Another member, my new roommate mother, picked me up from jail. Walking outside it was like a beautiful spring day, even in February. I felt spring inside, light, crisp and alive again.

Being at the mercy of people, because people can be so cruel. When you are at the mercy of people they imply that you'll never get on your feet. They feel if they don't treat you as such, you'll never leave or better yourself. They should come to you in a positive and constructive manner, not dogging me.

I was assigned another parole officer. I was back at square one, another year without violation before I could be removed from parole. Within a week I met my new parole officer. He was an older gentleman, very soft spoken Caucasian. He had many years under his belt as a parole officer, maturity; not a young rookie like my former parole officer.

I started back with my church, but it wasn't the same. However, I continued to be active in Sunday school, church services and night services. The attitudes of my fellow church goers was distant, like I had a contagious disease. I no longer fit into their group or class. I could feel the spirit as well as see it in their demeanour. My feelings of betrayal were valued, they were becoming my judge and executioner.

> "Judge not, that ye be not judged. (v1) For with what judgment ye judge, ye shall be judged: and with what measure ye mete, it shall be measured to you again. (v2) And why beholdest thou the mote that is in thy brother's eye, but considerest not the beam that is in thine own

eye?"
Matthew 7:1-3

Any church function, revivals, visiting churches, conferences, or activities, I was excluded from the program. I felt like an outsider. Was this the way Jesus would want the family of God to act? Certainly not.

I returned to Cal-State at Los Angeles, and re-enrolled in school to complete my degree. My original request for reenrolment was denied, based on the fact that I had abruptly left my classed without an official drop. I petitioned the admission's office stating the reasons and facts behind my departure. Taking into consideration my unusual circumstances. I was readmitted as a student. Subsequently, I had to reapply for the student aid and grants that I had lost due to my incarceration.

Two months after my release, I was still residing with my fellow church going friend, I received my first divorce settlement check.

During my marriage to Billy, I had amassed a net worth of 2.5 million in assets prior my incarceration. Not only did I not have my children with me, I had no choice but to settle for the meager pittance of $20,000.00 payable in instalments of $5,000.00 per month over four months.

Not having transportation other than public transportation, the city bus, I made a $2,000.00 down payment on a Hyundai. With funds left over, I began to search for a small store to open my own business. Within three weeks, I had located a small store off of Altadena Drive. It was perfect for Da'thy's, a ladies boutique shop, catering to Christian women. Within a week of securing the store, I moved into the back of the store. My permanent residence consisted of a ten by ten room. My pastor provided me with a couch which became a place to lay my head nightly over the next 2 1/2 years. I had a half bath, no shower or tub facilities, so I utilized family and friends shower and bath facilities. My source for cooking was a microwave oven. Times were hard. I had to economise in every way possible. I put in long hours. I was my own buyer; buying my inventory.

A carpenter worked at the layout of the store; shelving, a dressing room, a store closet, a room partition and a display rack. Four short weeks. I wanted to be ready for my grand opening.

I hired a part time sales clerk to manage the store while I was in school, and when I was at the swap meet. Two days a week I had secured a spot for each Wednesday and Saturday at the swap meet. On those days I would arrive at 5:00 A.M. with clothes and display racks.

Setting up the clothes and racks had to be organized for the 6:00 A.M. opening of the swap meet to the public.

By 2:00 P.M., I began the process of packing and tearing down the racks. These two days helped to advertise my business and financially secure my business with a positive cash flow.

Going through my mail I found an envelope from the A.F.D.C. appeals processing department. Looking at the envelop I was surprised. I assumed the time I had spent in jail that they would forget about my appeal on the Welfare fraud.

Legal Aid had done an excellent job for me in preparing and filling this appeal. Eighteen months later I was astounded when I read that the panel up held the fact that I had a right to receive A.F.D.C. for my teenage son, Louis, and that I hadn't abandon him, although we were temporarily apart.

Legal Aid help me prove the fact that I had not defrauded nor intended to defraud welfare. I had fallen into an emergency dilemma, and was legally within my rights. Here I was a day late, and a dollar short, because I had already served the time.

Coming home from school, my sales clerk gave me a message.

"Lance called."

"Lance called? What does he want?" I thought it was Lance senior.

"He says, he's your son, and he wants to talk to you!" the clerk said.

I had a feeling that something good had happened, I then said:

"He never calls. Where is his number?"

I was so elated. I began jumping around the boutique. I had a feeling something wonderful was happening. I had come to terms that we would never be a family unit. I'd be his mom, but he would be in Chicago living his lifestyle. Lance had been gone so long, five years.

"Give me the number, give me the number!"

Nervously I dialled his number. After three rings, I heard the click on the phone, then I heard soft voice answer.

"Hello?"

"Lance!" I said.

"Mom!" he yelled.

"Yes!" I answered.

"I'm ready to come home," he said.

"You can't come home! What about school?" I responded. It was January, Lance was in the middle of his senior year.

"I don't care about that mommy, I can't take it here anymore. Charles is unbearable," He explained.

I felt such a joy. My prayer had finally been answered regarding Lance. My son had come to the realization of his situation all by himself. This was a turning point in my faith, my prayers weren't in vain.

I asked him about all of his belongings.

"Lance, what about all your stuff, and your car?"

"I'm going to leave all of it and come home to you," he answered.

"Okay!" I said.

I sent him money overnight so he would be able to book his flight home. After securing a flight, Lance called to give me the information.

It was joyous. It was beyond my farthest expectations.

I called West, my friend from church. I informed her that my son, Lance, who I hadn't seen in about six years, was coming home to live with me.

"I want you to go to the airport with me. I probably won't recognize him. I didn't even recognize his voice on the phone. I don't have a picture of him," I confessed to her.

"You'll know him when you see him," she assured me.

I told her what time I'd pick her up on Wednesday.

So that Wednesday, we were off to L.A.X. Parking close to American Airline terminal. We headed toward the luggage claim, which is where I agreed to meet Lance.

The plan had landed by our arrival at the baggage claim, but the passengers had not deplaned as of yet. We stood anxiously taking and waiting for the passengers.

"This is one of the greatest days of my life!" I told West.

Descending from escalator, Lance walked through two double doors. Both West and I turned to see Lance with a carry-on luggage strapped over his shoulder. Running to embrace me, his limp wrist waving, he rushed over to me. His feminine actions surprised me. I had to tell myself not to be shocked. I must maintain a warmth and loving demeanour. I didn't want Lance to feel rejected. He was as handsome as ever, if not more so. Moving toward Lance, we met and embraced.

"Hi, mom! I'm so glad to see you!" he said

"Ah! This is such a wonderful day. You don't know what this means. You were the missing piece of the puzzle. Now the puzzle is complete," I said.

"I am so happy too, mommy!" he said.

"This is my friend, West," I said

Very politely, he shook West's hand. Being courteous, he escorted us across the street to my car, holding the door open for us. Such a gentleman.

We drove around to the curb so that Lance could pick up the remainder of his luggage. We drove back towards Pasadena, our home. During our drive, Lance went on to explain the terrible situation with Charles, how jealous and controlling he was, and how Lance's friends, his life, had become an emotional roller coaster: unmanageable, unbearable.

That following week, I enrolled Lance in John Muir High School as a senior. Right away, Lance was very popular. He was very outgoing and personable. His good looks landed him several dates for the upcoming prom. He was fitting in, right away, with many new friends.

He became a big asset to my business at the swap meet. His good looks attracted women. So my Saturdays at the swap meet were very profitable.

Our living arrangement at Da'thy's were not the norm. I slept on the couch in my back room, and Lance slept on a pallet in the dressing room. Each morning he'd roll up his pallet, storing it in the back room. This went on for the next two years. The situation of his spirit, Lance never complained.

He was never prideful, never being ashamed of our living conditions, just grateful that we were finally together under the same roof. Our time that we spent together was never dull. Lance's friends were always dropping by Da'thy's, all hours of the day and night. He gave out his telephone number like it was a business card.

Girls were always calling, finally I had to remind him.

"I'm not your secretary. This is a business, not a secretarial service!" I said.

"Al! Mon," his favorite expression, so carefree.

One day, Ann, a regular caller had maybe about fifteen times already that day. We had become telephone acquaintances, so she decided to pour out her heart to me.

"He never calls me back. He seldom calls me. My dad is upset because the phone bill is so high. I told him it was my boyfriend. Well, my daddy wants to meet Lance. We're having a family reunion and I invited Lance to come. I told my father he would meet Lance then. My father said if he can't meet this "guy" then I won't be able to make any more telephone calls on this phone."

This led me to ask Ann.

"Where do you live?"

"Compton," she replied

A frog went in my throat.

"Compton? Did you say Compton?"

"Yes!"

"Where did you meet Lance?" I asked.

"At the Queen Mary!" she said.

"Do you realize it would be too dangerous for him to come see you in Compton?" I questioned.

I couldn't talk anymore. Fear gripped my heart. I told her good-bye. There were gangs in that area. Lance could get killed. He had lived in a very affluent area of Chicago. He had never been exposed to gang violence. I didn't know if he ever knew of the troubling gang situation in California.

I couldn't sleep that night. I had to wait up for Lance. When he came home, we'd have to talk.

"Ann called today. She called about fifteen times. The last time we talked, she stated that she lived in Compton. She wanted you to come down to meet her family at a family reunion. Her father is upset with the high phone bills. Promise me! Promise me! Lance! Promise me! I plead, you won't go down there to see her! Do you know how dangerous it would be to go out to that area?"

"Ah! Mon!" his usual answer. "I can take care of myself."

"Lance, men get killed just by going into the area dating these young ladies," I told him.

"That's not going to happen to me!" he said.

"What makes you think you're exempt? Can't you get plenty of girls in this area? A lot of girls like you! Why do you want to go to Compton?"

"She is a nice girl, mon!" Lance said

"Okay! Lance, promise me! Please promise me, you will let this girl go. You'll leave her alone."

"Al, Mon! You're putting too much on it! Go to bed!" He exploded.

The following day I started my telephone campaign. I called anyone and everyone, my sisters, brothers, cousins, Lance's brothers and sisters. We had to talk him, trying to talk some sense into him. He didn't need to visit Compton, especially for a girl.

The telephone really began to ring for Lance. The calls were the same, trying to talk some sense about how dangerous his going to Compton could be. They advised him that he should listen to his mon. After three days of continuous telephone calls and well-meaning advice, Lance conceded.

"Okey mon! I won't go to Compton."

Victory was mine! Praise God!

Although I was virtuous in this situation with Ann, I still had much work to do on Lance's relationship with Janet. The first Sunday that Lance was with me, we attended my church. When the pastor gave an altar call, Lance stepped up. He gave his heart to Jesus. Bowering down on his knees in prayer, I was right at his side. Following our time together in prayer, Janet was present to assist Lance for further spiritual growth.

Following Janet into an upper-room to minister to him about the baptism of the Holy Spirit. Janet was a tall, but small framed woman, about 38 years old. A very plain Jane in looks, but was very spirit filled. A pillar of the church and a very active member for approximately ten years.

An hour after going into the upper room with Janet, Lance appeared in the sanctuary. His radiant smile and light step led me to believe that he had been baptized with the Holy Spirit. I embraced him, praising God for the miracle. That's why I had brought him to the church. A spiritual hospital to deliver him from any bad habits or bondage. I was so happy. Seeing the change in Lance, my mission was accomplished.

Never seeing Janet after their meeting, I didn't have the opportunity to thank her. Church services were over so we went out to have lunch and go home.

Arriving at home, within 30 minutes the phone rang. It was Janet for Lance. I felt this was appropriate as your spiritual counsellor, your mentor. They were supposed to help one develop in one's walk with the Lord. As there were women in the church than men, it was customary for an older women to discipline a young man. This wasn't out of the ordinary.

After a few telephone calls, I noticed that the conversations were more romantically inclined.

At that time I confronted Lance.

"The conversation that you and Janet had, well it seems like it is love related."

"Yeah mon, she has a love bug for me!" he said jokingly.

I then joked with my family about it. He had so many pretty young girls that he dated from high school. I couldn't imagine Lance giving Janet the time of day, as far as a love relationship. First of all, I thought he would be embarrassed because she was so plain in comparison to his other girlfriends. Besides she was old enough to be his mother.

Telling my family about this older lady of 38, chasing my 18 year old son, my oldest son, Lester, he hit the celling.

"Momma!" he'd screamed.

"That isn't funny. That old woman could ruin Lance!"

"Oh! Lester you're putting too much on it!" I said

"She's just attracted to him because he's so... good looking. If I wasn't his mother, I might be attracted to him, too!"

"Ah! Momma!" he screamed.

"You took him to church for help, and then she's coming on to him. She's out on line momma, she's out of line, and it isn't funny momma, it isn't funny at all!"

I could continue talking with Lester, but he was so upset. He wanted me to nip it in the bud. But I disagreed. I didn't want to blow it out of proportion. There was no sense in confronting Janet or the taking it to the pastor. I thought it would soon come to an end, or blow over.

"An old woman wanting a young man won't blow over momma!" Lester said.

"Okay! Lester, let it go. Let's just wait and see," I said.

Lance led me to believe it was a joke. He would be embarrassed with his friends, as popular as he was, to be with this old woman.

However, Janet was persistent. She kept calling and buying Lance gifts, sweaters, shirts, jeans, and shoes.

Lance was a very happy-go-lucky person. Janet caught him at a very vulnerable time. She pursued a relationship with Lance. She babied him like he was her only child. As time passed, Lance became dependent on Janet. Any time of the day or night, he could call her. She was always there for him. She always made sure Lance could contact her at any time. Lance knew her schedule, she made sure of it.

During a trip to New York to be a guest on a talk show, Lance dropped me off at Burbank Airport, and was to pick me up in two days. In this time frame he and a friend, each with a girlfriend, went to the park for a picnic.

His friend said, "Hey! Lance I left something in the car."

Having fun and not thinking much of it, Lance tosses his friend the car keys. Leaving Lance and the girls, he walks to the car and drove off.

After what seemed to be an extended period of time, his friend didn't return. Getting concerned, Lance leaves the girls with the picnic and goes to see what could be taking his friend so long.

But the car was gone and his friend also. His friend is nowhere to be found. Returning to the girls, he lets them know that the car was gone.

Waiting a few hours, they surmised he had gone to the store. When he never returned, Lance realized his friend had stolen the car. The girls decided to call the police and report the car was stolen.

Lance felt so bad. This was our only source of transportation. It was our livelihood. I used the car for going to school, going to the swap meet, and picking up clothes for Da'thy's. He also realized he had to pick me up from the airport.

Having no other option, he had to call Janet. She was right there to help him through this crisis. He was emotionally vulnerable at this point. Janet drove her car with Lance to the airport. Pleading his case, he proceeded to tell me about the incident. Janet offered to be my taxi until I got the car back. Janet defended Lance's position. She had struck gold with Lance.

After this incident, Janet proved her loyalty to Lance. This was what clinched their budding relationship. I knew then what was going on. I attempted to dissuade him from pursuing this relationship. His friends tried to talk him out of having an affair with Janet, to no avail.

I called Janet and requested that she come by the boutique, so we could talk.

"The reason for this meeting is to talk about Lance. Lance has been through a traumatic experience for someone his age. And when he came to live with me, it was a new beginning in his life. This relationship that you are having does not help the problem. Would you please stop seeing him? He is just a kid! He has so much hurt inside of him that needs to be healed, and with you around him, it can't be healed."

Janet responded, "He is a kid in age, but he is a man in mind!"

"He is not a man. He is a little country boy!" I said

"Oh! Well, we get along so wonderful!" she explained.

"Yeah, but I am not happy because of that. You're pimping him, so you think I am happy about that? You give him everything he asks for. You think I want that for him?" I asked.

"Well, I'll see what he has to say!" she answered.

She then stood up and walked out of the store. Knowing that Janet would not comply with what I had pleaded with her, I had no other choice but to call the pastor.

Calling the pastor I explained the situation and duration of time this relationship had gone on. He expressed his disappointment in Janet, but he wasn't surprised when I called. But pastor wasn't surprised at her actions. He already knew that they were involved.

Pastor called Janet and requested a face to face meeting at the church office. He spoke with her about the relationship. He reminded her that she was on the ministry staff. Her behaviour and manner in which she conducted herself was critical to the church.

Janet refused to stop seeing Lance. Shortly thereafter, Lance and I left the church, joining a church in Los Angeles. Soon thereafter, Janet left the church, joining a church in Altadena, after the pastor had relieved her of her ministerial duties.

Even though, we were attending another church, Janet continued to seek out her relationship with Lance. Three years into their relationship, against the family's wishes, Lance moved into Janet's apartment.

I had to call a truce.

"Let's stop blaming Janet for the relationship. It's just as much Lance's desire as it is Janet's. He wants this relationship. Let's be thankful it's a woman. Let us accept it. He wants her. Don't treat her with a cold shoulder any more, and don't accuse her anymore of robbing the cradle," I preached.

Soon thereafter, Lance and I went to visit Lesa at her house. In the car, I told Lance that I had a family meeting. I told everyone to let your relationship with Janet be, because, this is what you wanted also. We're all going to accept her as your girlfriend. Then I went on to say:

"Please Lance, don't make her my daughter-in-law! Please don't marry her!"

"I'm am not going to marry her, mom, but the girl I marry has got to treat me like Janet does," he said.

"Lance! A young woman isn't going to have to treat you like Janet does. Do you realize Janet treats you like that because she is old enough to be your mother?"

"Yes! There is one out there that will treat me like Janet does!" he shouted.

"A young woman is not going to put up with the things that Janet does. You'll have to condition your mind to remember that. You can't be no player, and keep a good woman," I preached.

After a three year relationship, Lance moved into Janet's apartment, as her lover, but within the year, approaching New Year's Day, Janet had wanted to spend New Year's Eve with Lance. He had other plans. Janet believed that this would bring her good-luck, spending New Year's Eve with the man she loved. Lance continued to see other women, although he resided with Janet. Lance had planned to spend the evening with Janet after their argument.

However, early evening Janet attended a New Year's Eve church service, so to be home with Lance at mid-night. While she was at church, Lance's friend Jim, called and invited him out for an evening with the girls and guys.

"I promised Janet I would spend the night with her," he responded.

"Don't be a stick in the mud. It's New Year's Eve. Let's celebrate!" Jim said.

Convincing Lance, he proceeded to get dressed for Jim to pick him up. Janet arrived home as Lance was preparing for his night out with his friends. Wondering why he was always stressed, they were to spend a quiet evening at home alone, a candlelight dinner and watching the countdown on New Year's.

Lance advised Janet that there was a change in plans. He was going to spend New Year's with his friends. Jim arrived. Blocking the door, Janet was crying. Lance pushed her aside, and stepped outside to greet his friend, Jim. Walking to Jim's car, they turned to see Janet running toward them with a knife in her hand.

Fury written all over her face, like she was possessed by the devil. This was the first time Lance was afraid of her even though they had had words before. She was like a wild animal. Fearing for his life, that night he made up his mind that he was cutting her loose. The relationship was over.

While Janet was at work, Lance returned to pick up his personal belongings. He rented his own apartment. Got a job at the hospital to support himself.

During his tenure at the hospital he met his future wife. Two years after meeting they married and had a baby girl. They now live in Utah and are living happily ever after.

During our residing in the back room of Da'thy's, we always had excitement. One evening after we had closed the store, Lance had made plans to go out. He went out almost every night. Leaving the store, he would always lock the exterior burglar door. The door was made of wrought iron bars.

At about 1:00 A.M., I was awakened by a loud burst of noise, as if someone had fallen against the door. Looking at the clock, I figured it was Lance.

Getting out of bed I said to myself:

"That boy has gone out and got drunk! Falling all over the place."

Sitting up, stumbling to the front of the store with sleep in my eyes, I yelled:

"Lance! Lance! Boy, what is wrong with you?"

Looking up, within arm's reach stood a burglar. The burglar looked like something from fright night. Fear overtook him. Like lighting, he ran like a bat out of hell. Running for his life down the street was an awesome sight. He may have frightened me, but I believe I frightened him more.

Returning back inside the store, I telephoned the police. Shortly after completing the report, Lance arrived at the scene. The police chastised him for leaving the burglar door unlocked.

"Ah! Momma! I am so sorry. Thank you God nothing happened. I'm so happy you're not hurt. If you had been hurt, I don't know what I would have done. I love you mom."

CHAPTER 9

Family Reunification

> "Thus saith the Lord; a voice was heard in Ra'mah, lamentation and bitter weeping; Rahel weeping for her children refused to be comforted for her children because they were not. (v.15) Thus saith the Lord; refrain thy voice from weeping, and thine eyes from tears; for thy work shall be rewarded, saith the Lord, and they shall come again from the land of the enemy. (v.16) And there is hope in thine end, saith the Lord that thy children shall come again to their own border."
> **Jeremiah 31:15-17**

Having not seen my children since our last flu visit in February 1986, three months prior to my release from prison, I decided to seek legal help. In February 1988, I had scheduled a consultation with my first attorney.

Her review of the divorce decree: it was determined it would be impossible to have the decree overturned as far as the custody of the children. Billy had sole custody, as if I didn't exist. All I wanted was equal custody. I didn't want to take the children from their father. I only wanted to see them and have visitation rights.

Due to shrewdness of his attorneys, I was advised that it would cost $20,000.00 just to see what she could do.

I felt betrayed by Billy. I felt hurt. I didn't go to jail for being an unfit mother, but for bringing money into the family, so we could live better.

I became a victim of the system, which is blind, dumb, deaf, crippled, and crazy.

In speaking with my nephew, he introduced me to a private attorney in Century City, an attorney for the stars. The cream of the crop attorney. After reviewing the same paper work, he determined that there was no judge in the nation who was going to change this order. Billy had a six bedroom house, with six bathrooms, in an affluent area of Las Vegas, as well as two businesses.

"No judge is going to uproot those children. You just got out of prison. You have nothing, no leg to stand on!" was his reply.

He advised me to let it go. There was nothing that could possibly be done. Thank goodness, the consultation was free! Strike two.

My third consultation was a repeat of one and two. My fourth strike was different, leaving the paperwork with a lawyer, for his review. I waited patiently for over two months for his determination of the situation. He never called, nor returned my calls. He never even returned the degree. Strike four!

My fifth strike: I gave an attorney $1,000.00. He said he could put into action the necessary motions to have the decree overturned. With my $1,000.00 receipt in hand, I left his office, happy, like I was finally getting somewhere. Another year had passed. It was now 1989.

Calling to get a status on my case, I was always advised he was never available, but he would call me back. He never did. Over a three to four month time frame, I decided to write him personally, in hopes of getting his attention. My correspondence was never acknowledged. It was like corresponding with the dead.

Feeling drained, I felt it was no use in pursuing this any further. Some of the pillars of the church gave me various advice.

"Just go get your children!" was the most common advice.

However, a few members suggested, that I forget about my children. My heart was telling me about the children: it said my children was coming home; don't give up.

I began fasting and praying more about my children. Pretty soon they would all be grown. One night I was longing for my children. I lay paralyzed when an unexpected fear overcame me. I was afraid that my own children would never seek me out, their own mother. I was panic stricken by that thought.

Getting up, I prayed on my knees. Through my tears, I cried out to the Lord:

"Why is this happening to me? Why can't I get my kids? This attorney has taken the money I had! Why is this happening to me? You gave me those kids! I birthed them. Why are you going to let someone take them? I don't know any lawyer! They are all afraid of the state of California. They act like the state of California is God, but you are God!"

Still on my knees in front of the couch I felt a heat wave, but the heat was more intense, not that of my tears. I heard a voice:

"Stop crying! Your children are coming home!"

Standing up I exclaimed to air:

"I can't bring them here. I don't have a place to bring to! I ain't got no money to pay a lawyer!"

The calming voice encouraged me:

"You do it!"

Sitting down I began to think: "Well, I see papers that lawyers file. I could write something like that."

The following day I called my daughter, Lesa. I told her the Lord had spoken to me through the window. I said:

"I really do feel I can do it. I can forget about lawyers. I can do it!"

Lesa encouraged me.

"If the Lord told you to do it momma, I believe you can do it."

Later that day, I began my research at the local library: how to file custody papers for my children in addition to a small claims motion against my attorney who robbed me of my $1,000.00

Two weeks later, I filed both motions. The small claims was filed in Pasadena, the custody motion with the Superior Court in Los Angeles.

Within sixty days, I had appeared before both courts. The small claims court granted my judgement against the attorney. The custody filing in Superior Court was denied. The judge stated:

"Mrs. Woods, I 'm not saying that you don't have a valid argument. Your paperwork is not correct. You don't have all the necessary legal documents. Case dismissed."

Not continuing the case, I had to start all over, including another filing fee. I felt deflated, devastated and abused by the system. Before leaving the courtroom, the clerk, beckoned Lance over to her desk.

"Tell your mother all is not lost, don't give up. There are some forms downstairs that she needs to file with her complaint. Have the law clinics check her paperwork before filing next time," she said.

Walking out of the courtroom, Lance relayed the clerk advice.

"Lance, it's no use. I'm always running into a dead end!" I cried.

"Ah! Mon! Trust me it's worth it. It's worth it! It's worth it! I'll be by your side until we get the kids!" he said.

It took two weeks for me to compile the paperwork again, including the additional forms the clerk had mentioned. The law clinic in Glendale reviewed the paperwork for accuracy. Again, I had to pay the $175.00 filing fee.

Two and a half months later, we came before the court. A female judge was assigned this time. I felt this judge could identify with being a mother, and wanting to be with your children.

Billy was served through the marshal's office in Las Vegas. He ignored the summons, believing that California had no jurisdiction of him. I was fighting air. The judge granted a continuance for sixty days giving Billy the benefit of the doubt in that maybe he would respond.

Sixty days later, Billy was a no show again, knowing full well that he was in receipt of the summons. The court notified him, that he was in contempt of court for failing to appear. He was advised that the children were still under the jurisdiction of California until they were eighteen years of age.

Ninety days later, were back in court. Billy and his wife had seated themselves in the rear of the courtroom. I walked in, wearing a business suit, my brief case, sharp like an attorney, very polished, and sitting in a position of authority close to the front of the courtroom.

Calling my case before the judge, Billy walks up, with a smile on his face, as if he had an easy victory. Billy seated himself at the right conference table, I was at the left. Sitting down, I opened my briefcase, taking out my motion paperwork and divorce decree. The judge reviewed her case paperwork.

"Mr. Woods, I see here Mrs. Woods hasn't been with her children in seven years. She is requesting to see her children, and modify the custody decision to equal rights. So what do you have to say about that?" she stated.

Sitting from his chair, bracing himself, then leaning forward, he said:

"Well, your Honor, the kids don't want anything to do with her! They said if they have to leave me, and made to have anything to do with her, they're going to kill themselves. She's a jailbird! She has a bad behaviour, and besides, Judge, she has no way of taking care of them. She has no place to stay. She has no place herself!"

Glaring at me, he reminded me of Judas Iscariot, condemning me. Turning to me, the Judge said:

"What do you have to say about that?"

"Your Honor, in reference to point number one, if he believed that the children would kill themselves if they had to stay with anyone but him, let him die tonight, and see if they would join him!"

Bolting in his seat, he looked like I had passed a death sentence on him. He became rigid.

"Your Honor, if the children said that, it must be the environment they live in. They have to call their stepmother "Mother", they can't even call my name in the house. They have to pretend that she gave them birth. In reference to point number three, Mr. Woods claims I have no place to live. Well, people have not stopped making houses and apartments. They still rent houses and apartments. If the Lord put it in your heart, your Honor, to give me equal custody of the children, he will provide a place for them to live!" I answered.

With that, the Judge said:

"I tell you what I'm going to do. I'm going to have you see a court mediator, and have her work out the conditions between the two of you. Then I will give you a year's trial period to see how the children adjust to you and your situation. Come back at 3:00 P.M. today so I can review the conditions."

"Thank you, your honour."

So we started to work on the plan that the mediator worked out for us. We started right away. The children came to see me right away. They stayed a weekend because they were in school. Then the next weekend, I went to Las Vegas to visit them. Every month, I continuously visit them since they were still in school.

At the end of the school year, the children came to stay with me for a month. Before going back to Las Vegas, the oldest girl wanted to stay with me and go to school. The judge granted her request, so she stayed with me and was very happy. We went to church together on Sundays. After that year, the second daughter wanted to come to stay with me and go to school as well. The judge granted her request, too.

Then I finished college and applied for a loan and was approved. I rented my first house, and opened a Lady's clothing. I made lots of money. I then purchased a house in San Bernardino because I wanted something better for my girls. The other two came to stay with me.

The author earned her degree in sociology and has been a minister for nineteen years as well as the president of an Outreach. She has owned her own business and has published her autobiography, *The Welfare Queen*. The author loves to write and currently resides in California.

www.ingramcontent.com/pod-product-compliance
Lightning Source LLC
LaVergne TN
LVHW041541060526
838200LV00037B/1082